THE LIGHT IN BETWEEN

MARELLA CARACCIOLO CHIA

THE LIGHT IN BETWEEN

Translated from the Italian
by Howard Curtis

PUSHKIN PRESS

First published in Italian as
Una Parentesi Luminosa © Adelphi 2008

English translation © Howard Curtis 2010

This edition first published in 2010 by
Pushkin Press
12 Chester Terrace
London NW1 4ND

British Library Cataloguing in Publication Data:
A catalogue record for this book is available
from the British Library

ISBN 978 1 906548 27 8

Cover Illustration: *Sunlight* 1909 Frank Weston Benson
© Indianapolis Museum of Art John Herron Fund

Frontispiece: *Portrait of Vittoria Colonna*
reproduced by kind permission of Vittoria and Selina Bonelli Zondadari

Set in 10.5 on 13.5 Baskerville Monotype
and printed in Great Britain on Munken Premium White 90 gsm
by TJ International Ltd

www.pushkinpress.com

THE LIGHT IN BETWEEN

Prologue

October 2006

For some years I had been researching a story which particularly intrigued me—the story of Leone Caetani, Fifteenth Duke of Sermoneta and husband of Vittoria Colonna. Why, in May 1921, at the age of fifty-one, did this traveller and orientalist, a respected member of the Accademia dei Lincei as well as a member of the Italian parliament from 1909 to 1913, abandon everything—his wife, his son, the vast estates inherited from his family and a massive work, destined to remain unfinished, on the origins of Islam—and leave Rome with a young woman named Ofelia Fabiani and their daughter for Vernon, a pioneer town in the Okanagan Mountains of Western Canada, where he spent the last fourteen years of his life in a small house on the edge of a wood? What could have driven him, I wondered, to make such a radical gesture, to abandon all the things which up until that point had given his life form and meaning?

For years, I had been searching for the correspondence between Leone and Vittoria: in the Caetani archives in Rome and at Tor Tre Ponti in the Pontine Plain; in the Leone Caetani Foundation of the Accademia dei Lincei, and in the Colonna archive at the monastery of Subiaco to the east of Rome, but to no avail. I knew it existed—there were references to it in other letters by Vittoria—but it appeared to be lost. I had even gone to Canada to look through Leone's papers, but in vain.

Then, in the autumn of 2006, I approached Prospero Colonna, the grandson of a cousin of Vittoria's. "I think I can help you," he said, and told me about a trunk that the princess had left his father which had been opened a few months before our conversation. "We took a look in the trunk," Prospero went on, "and as it contained a lot of letters from Vittoria to her husband, we decided to give the whole thing to the Caetani archive in Rome."

The Caetani archive, which contains thousands of documents covering more than a millennium of Roman history, is on the second floor of the sixteenth-century Palazzo Caetani in the centre of Rome. Both the palace and the archive belong to a foundation that bears the name of the last male descendant of the family—Camillo Caetani, the son of Leone's younger brother Roffredo and the American Marguerite Chapin, whose death on the Albanian front in 1940, at the age of twenty-five, had marked the end of the dynasty.

The reading room of the Caetani library is dark and smells of paper and beeswax. Passing me the boxes containing the rediscovered correspondence, the curator of the archive asked me to handle the letters carefully, as I was the first person to examine them in more than half-a-century. The last to do so before me had been Vittoria herself. At some point, when she was old and alone, the princess must have felt a pressing need to put the scattered fragments of her life into some kind of order, and had decided to safeguard a major part of it.

She had put all the letters in a trunk, locked it and entrusted it to a cousin whom she knew she could rely on. There was one condition—that it should not be opened for any reason until fifty years after her death. Her wish was respected.

The sheer amount of material left by the princess was impressive. There was, for example, a long manuscript in which Vittoria had given an account of her life since the Great War. There were many invitations, like that sent on behalf of King

Edward VII of England, asking her to spend a few days with him and the Queen at Windsor Castle. There were also invitations to the theatre, to balls and to receptions at the Quirinale, where she was a lady-in-waiting to Queen Elena.

But, above all, there were the letters which Vittoria had written to Leone during a twenty-year marriage marked by constant separations, and which she had clearly managed to retrieve. There were thousands of them in bundles tied with blue gauze ribbons, each bundle corresponding to a year. They covered the whole history of Vittoria and Leone's relationship, from its birth at Ninfa in the spring of 1901 all the way to its epilogue in 1921, when Leone—who had become Duke of Sermoneta four years earlier—left for Canada with his new family.

Suddenly, as I looked through this mountain of paper and ink, I discovered a bundle that seemed different from the rest, being tightly bound with string. I opened it as gently and carefully as I could. What I discovered was a group of twenty-one letters. On many of the pages, I recognised Vittoria's broad, rounded handwriting, and some of them also bore her monogram: a *V* and a *C* in an oval surrounded by swirling bands and surmounted by a princely crown. There were other letters, too, long ones with a great many deletions, all signed in the same way: "Your Boccioni."

The bundle also contained a few photographs: Vittoria standing in a garden, surrounded by hydrangeas; Vittoria on a balcony looking out at the lake; Vittoria strolling, accompanied by a large dog wagging its tail. They had all been taken during the same period—July 1916. There was also a tiny photo of Boccioni, with his athletic body and elegant attire, in his Milanese studio, beside the plaster cast of his sculpture *Spiral Expansion of Muscles in Motion.* Another photograph showed him standing in his military uniform, an ironic smile on his handsome face. Between two of the letters, I also found a linen handkerchief, folded in four, with an embroidered border and no initials. This small piece of material must have belonged to Umberto Boccioni—probably made for him by his mother, the elderly seamstress who appears in so many of her son's paintings and drawings.

The Boccioni-Colonna correspondence immediately struck me as being of exceptional interest. Without hesitation, I put aside (at least temporarily) my researches into Leone Caetani and set about trying to reconstruct, as far as was possible, the encounter that gave rise to those letters.

What follows is the story of that encounter.

Vittoria riding her bicycle near Villa Borghese in Rome (c 1900)

O N THE MORNING OF the seventh of June 1916, Vittoria Colonna Caetani, who had arrived a few days earlier on the Isolino di San Giovanni, a small island on Lake Maggiore, woke up early. The damp, cool air coming into her bedroom suggested that yet another storm was on its way. In that second year of the war, it was as if the summer really did not want to arrive, but Vittoria did not care. She had plenty of little projects and everyday actions to fill her days in the peace and quiet of the Isolino.

First of all, she had to finish furnishing the room on the ground floor, a tiny room with windows looking out across the lake to the mountains of Switzerland. After all, sooner or later Leone—who, although he was already forty-seven and was deeply opposed to Italy's entry into the war, had enlisted as a volunteer—might decide to take a few days leave on the Isolino with his wife and son, perhaps to celebrate their fifteenth wedding anniversary, which would fall on the twentieth of that month. There, in that little room directly above the water, like the cabin of a yacht, Leone might be able to lose himself in his books just as he did in his library at Palazzo Caetani in Rome.

The vases in the drawing room had to be filled with fresh flowers—Vittoria always liked to have the house full of flowers—and she had to come to a decision with the gardener as to where to build the hen house. In addition, the plants she had ordered from Mr Curtis' famous nurseries on the Riviera had arrived, and Vittoria absolutely had to decide where to put them today. "I'm in the garden every morning before nine and there's so much to do, I don't have a moment's rest all day!" she had written a few days earlier to Leone, who was with his regiment in the mountains on the border with Austria.

Vittoria's life on her beloved Isolino was clearly very different from the social whirl that dominated her life during the winter months, when she divided her time between Rome, London and Paris. Even in Monte Carlo, where she had just taken a holiday and where—despite the grim atmosphere of the war— she had gambled every evening with her friend the Aga Khan and a small group of European aristocrats, Vittoria had been forced to resort to her usual drops of veronal, the powerful barbiturate that calmed her nerves and helped her to sleep. "Modern women keep going with the help of poisons," she had once written to her husband after an excessive dose had confined her to bed for three days.

That morning on the Isolino, a Wednesday, Vittoria woke before eight. She was wearing one of her elegant nightdresses, perhaps the pink silk one with the "wonderful little bonnet" bought a couple of weeks earlier during her stay on the Côte d'Azur. Emma, the chambermaid, placed a silver tray with a cup and a steaming pot of coffee on the table next to her bed and opened the curtains and shutters over the two windows. The newly painted walls of the bedroom reflected the morning light, and, sitting up in her wide bed, supported on a pile of goose-down pillows, Vittoria could see—beyond the dark shadows of the camphors and redwoods—the shimmering reflection of the sky in the blue-grey water of the lake.

The leisurely morning ritual of drinking coffee and reading the newspapers got under way. At that time, in the mountains of Trentino where Leone's regiment was stationed, the Italian forces were retreating under heavy Austrian artillery fire. The Russians, meanwhile, were massing troops on the Romanian front in preparation for a massive attack on Austria. "The arrival of the newspaper is an emotional moment," Vittoria wrote to her husband. "For a while it only carried bad news, but now the brave Russians are filling my heart."

That seventh of June, Vittoria was expecting a special visitor—the futurist painter and sculptor Umberto Boccioni, whom she had met the previous day at Villa San Remigio, on the eastern shore of the lake, at the house of her neighbours Silvio and Sofia della Valle di Casanova. She had taken an immediate liking to the thin, dark young man a few years her junior. His inquisitive, sensitive eyes and his smile, always ready to turn into ironic, contagious laughter, had made an agreeable impression on her. Before lunch, they had walked on the terrace, where Boccioni had set up his easel in the shade of an oak to work on his portrait of Ferruccio Busoni. The Casanovas called this terrace 'the belvedere' because of its view of the lake and the Alps. From it, it was possible to see the outline of the Isolino, with the old bell tower and the pink tiles appearing above the thick foliage. "My floating garden" was how Vittoria referred to her island. That little luxuriant, round piece of land, a few metres from the shore of Pallanza, had so intrigued Boccioni that he had asked if he could come there the following day and explore it with her.

Vittoria Colonna took particular care in choosing what to wear that day. For years, she had learnt to hide her deep emotional insecurity—"Love me because I need it," she had written to Leone a few weeks before meeting Boccioni, "I am the loneliest person in this world"—behind a façade of couture clothes bought from the most celebrated dressmakers in London and Paris, jewellery, silk stockings, soft leather shoes and hats. For Boccioni's visit, Vittoria would wear a white dress, or at least something very light in colour, which would bring out her suntanned complexion—skin "like a Creole", she called it. She rearranged the dark, wavy hair that framed her fine, stern face, enhancing her chestnut eyes and perfect white teeth.

Then, still in her gardening clothes, she descended the steps of the villa's grand staircase which had been embellished recently with a cloth runner in an attempt to prettify the spartan interiors of the former convent. In order not to ruin it, all the occupants of the villa (apart from her unmanageable fourteen-year-old son Onorato) had to contrive a comical way of climbing and descending the thin strips of stone at the sides of the cloth, keeping close either to the wall or to the handrail, which made them seem, Vittoria wrote, like "acrobats dancing on a rope".

The English-style breakfast (tea, eggs, toast and orange marmalade) was served on the balcony, from where she and her son Onorato could gaze at the snow-capped peaks of the Alps. The air was dense with rain, which made the smells all the more intense—the resin in the tree trunks, the cut grass, the earth. After giving Gertie (her faithful English governess, who, a few weeks earlier, had married Italo Donnini, a handyman also employed by the Caetanis) her instructions for the day, Vittoria left the house. Max, a young dog with wolf's blood, ran to her, and "together [they] walked around the garden". In the green tranquillity of the Isolino, the fear of war receded into the darkest, remotest corners of the mind, making way for other things. "I am delighted by my roses which are coming along really well," Vittoria had written to Leone as soon as she had set foot on the Isolino again a few days earlier, "and what I'm trying to do is to make the island even more beautiful for that great day when you can live on it with me." In her basket, she had what she needed: pruning shears, gardening gloves and a tattered copy of *The Complete Gardener*.

The sky, in that wartime June, was strangely unsettled, full of clouds and storms, but the mood in the house was light, especially as they were expecting Emilio, the Caetanis' chauffeur, to arrive in Pallanza that day with a new automobile: an Overland for Vittoria. At about eleven, the princess went back into the house and devoted herself to her correspondence. The first letter, as always, was for her husband, and as always (or almost always, as we shall see) began "My darling".

Darling, I haven't written to you for three days, I've been somewhat discouraged by the fact that my letters never seemed to arrive, and was beginning to doubt that the address was sufficient.

Then, after expressing her joy at the fact that Leone—who was at Calalzo, not far from the front—was leading a healthy, active life in the mountains and was not in danger for the moment, she told him in her usual light-hearted, nonchalant tone about the events of the previous day, including the apparently insignificant encounter which, within a few weeks, would turn their life upside down.

Yesterday I had lunch at the Casanovas', who have as their guests the pianist Busoni and the Futurist Boccioni: the latter is painting the former's portrait: I can't tell you what it's like!! Busoni seems to me something of a poseur; what is called a fine-looking man, and he never forgets it for a minute. Boccioni is much friendlier, a 'jolly boy', full of joy and intelligence. He's coming to see the island today: he will find it very old-fashioned! Tant pis pour lui. *I like it the way it is.*

Umberto Boccioni, who had originally been expected at Villa San Remigio on the twenty-first of May, had finally arrived more than two weeks late. Constant changes of plan, second thoughts and various complications—including several days of sickness at the end of May—had prevented him from leaving Milan.

"The house and the grounds are a fine work of art," the fifty-year-old Ferruccio Busoni had written to him on the thirty-first of May, in an attempt to goad his young friend to join him as soon as possible. The villa and the garden were "the result of thirty years of care and planning. The terraces tower above the lake as

19

if it belonged to them. The whole place is utopian and, if you like, rather artificial and—without being fantastic—dreamlike."

There was indeed something in the nature of a dream about the villa and the vast garden which surrounded it, a dream of a somewhat sentimental nature, being the culmination of the love between Silvio della Valle di Casanova—a nobleman of Neapolitan origin but central European culture—and his wife, the Irish-born Sofia (Sophie) Browne. He was a poet and musician and an eclectic collector, and she a painter and an enthusiastic gardener. Being first cousins, they had known each other for ever, but had married late and had one daughter, Esther. Villa San Remigio, where they lived all year round, was the result of their passion, which, perhaps for reasons of modesty, they had preferred to keep secret for decades.

The villa is located at the top of the Colle della Castagnola, at Verbania Pallanza, about five hundred metres, as the crow flies, from the Isolino. Today—stripped of its original furnishings to make way for administrative offices—it is an empty shell. The grounds, on the other hand, are still very much as they were when Boccioni saw them, when they were carefully tended by the Marchesa di Casanova and a staff of thirty, including gardeners, plumbers and artisans.

By the beginning of June 1916, as we have seen, Ferruccio Busoni was growing impatient for his young friend to come to this temple to the sentiments, an old-fashioned place par excellence, as Marinetti would have defined 'old-fashioned': that is, "static, traditional, pessimistic, pacifist, nostalgic, decorative and aesthetic", in other words, anti-Futurist. It could certainly be boring, and the artificial atmosphere of Villa San Remigio got on Busoni's nerves. Like Boccioni, he preferred the chaos, noise and vitality of a big city to the silence of the country. "I could not bear such an environment for very long," he had written, threateningly, to his friend who was still taking his time.

Umberto Boccioni finally arrived at San Remigio on the fourth of June, a Sunday, joining Busoni and his Swedish wife Gerda

Sjöstrand as a guest of the Casanovas. His intention was to stay three weeks. He was excited at the prospect of doing a portrait of Maestro Busoni, who, in spite of the war, had just returned from a highly successful concert tour of Europe. In a letter sent to Busoni at the beginning of April, Boccioni had declared that he was "extremely happy to please you and flattered that my art should be so desired by you!" The friendship between Busoni and Boccioni dated from 1912, when the composer had bought *The City Rises*. Since then, although they had only seen each other four times, they had kept in touch and Busoni had bought other paintings, including *Mourning*.

But Boccioni was anxious, too. He did not know if the impatient, occasionally quick-tempered Busoni would be willing to sit for hours in the open air posing for him: " … I can tell you I was very afraid you would resist … " he would write to him once the portrait was finished. "I know what it means to wait and see other people work." He was equally anxious at the thought of having a demanding subject who was also a paying customer and someone who would be watching him closely in what was a return to painting after a long period of absence.

Umberto Boccioni had not, in fact, spent the last six months of 1915 surrounded by colours and brushes, but at the front. A convinced interventionist (as indeed was Vittoria Colonna) he had enlisted, along with the other members of the Futurist group, in the Lombard Volunteer Cyclist Battalion. He had left for the front in July, and in October had taken part, together with his friend Marinetti, the architect Antonio Sant'Elia and the artists Anselmo Bucci and Mario Sironi, in the famous capture of Dosso Casina, not far from Lake Garda. "All we eat is a little bread and a little canned meat," he wrote in his war notebook on the twenty-fifth of October 1915. "We carry on our work amid heavy fire. Every time a shell whizzes past, we run behind a stone with our heads down. We are dirty, ragged and exhausted. We haven't washed our faces or hands for five or six days. But we go on! The nights are terribly windy. Our feet are so cold, they stop us from sleeping. About midnight, Sironi comes to me and, lying close together with our legs intertwined, we try to sleep. Impossible."

Having returned to Milan for a long leave (the Lombard Volunteer Cyclist Battalion had been disbanded in December 1915) Boccioni had spent the first months of 1916, as he wrote in a letter to Busoni, "absolutely overwhelmed by things to do". Apart from photographing and cataloguing his works and sending some to various buyers, Boccioni had followed a general knowledge course in preparation for exams to become a second lieutenant. In addition, he had spent much of his time organising a sculpture exhibition to be held in Milan at the end of May, the proceeds from which would be used to help families of the wounded and prisoners of war. "All the preparations are on my shoulders and it isn't a small thing, or amusing."

Boccioni was quite pleased, therefore, to leave Milan in June. He needed to put a certain distance between himself and the Futurist movement and to mitigate the tension of the last few months. Squabbles with some of his artist friends and with the gallery owner, by "offending [his] dignity", as he wrote to Busoni, drove him to withdraw from the exhibition at the last moment. Even the war, which at first had seemed like a great adventure, now loomed heavily over his life and his desire to return to work. "My levy hasn't yet been called," he wrote in April to Ferruccio Busoni. "Who knows if we'll have time to work at San Remigio? I'm working in a very irregular way. I don't feel calm. The next call to arms is making me indecisive. I'm glad, of course, to be serving my country again even though it's doing me enormous harm."

Once he had finally arrived, Boccioni was happy to fall under the spell of the Casanovas' aesthetic excesses. And although he complained in a letter about the studied lack of electric light at

Villa San Remigio ("Candles, candles, candles"), he was really enthusiastic about his room and his huge four-poster bed with its canopy of yellow brocade. Sleeping in it, he wrote, made him feel like Cesare Borgia. In addition, the Casanovas' late-nineteenth-century eclecticism amused him and distracted him from thoughts of the war.

"The villa here is quite spectacular," he wrote to his brother-in-law Guido Callegari soon after his arrival. " … Huge rooms with stucco and gilding. Massive antique furniture, chests of all kinds, precious missals, highly worked wooden thrones. Hundreds of inlaid cupboards, dozens of suits of armour, hundreds of spears, daggers, pistols. In short, three hundred years of devoted collecting, old-fashioned but quite tasteful." He was particularly struck by the abundance of space. One of the drawing rooms of the villa, devoted to old weapons, he notes with astonishment, was large enough to hold five hundred people. Even the dining room, with its gilded arches beneath which musicians sometimes played—and where "the servants serve in silence"—was vast. But the thing that most astonished Umberto Boccioni about the Villa San Remigio was the combination of luxury and simplicity: "a simplicity without labels, without formality".

After studying the way the morning light changed in the garden, Boccioni immediately set to work. The place he had selected for Busoni to pose was a far cry from the sentimentality of the garden. The Maestro was to sit at the corner of a low wall, in the shade of a tree with a light-coloured trunk and big round leaves, perhaps a plane tree or a magnolia grandiflora, with his back to the lake and the mountains, almost as a kind of intellectual rejection of the romanticism that dominated the Casanovas' aesthetic.

During the breaks, Boccioni would lean on the low wall of the terrace—the same one on which he had posed Busoni, and which can be glimpsed in the portrait—and smoke a cigarette. From here, he had a magnificent view of the lake and the whole area, which for centuries had constituted the feudal domain of the powerful Borromeo family.

Even today, if you stand on the belvedere and face south, you can clearly see the outlines of the Borromean Islands. To the right, not far from the Stresa shore, is the fabulous silhouette of Isola Bella, its baroque terraces and high walls floating on the water like a majestic ship. Closer to you is Isola Madre, with its sixteenth-century palace surrounded by an oasis of exotic plants populated by white peacocks and other rare birds. On a clear day, you can also see the little Isola dei Pescatori, with its colourful houses and the boats in its small harbour. Finally, if you look down, beyond the wooded shore at the bottom end of the garden, you glimpse the smallest of the Borromean Islands, the dense, mysterious, unfathomable Isolino di San Giovanni.

It seems quite likely that either Sofia Casanova or her husband, strolling with Umberto Boccioni in the garden soon after his arrival, would have drawn his attention to the fact that a Roman princess lived on that tiny island, a princess bearing the same name as her ancestor, the poet who had been Michelangelo's muse and correspondent. This would surely have caught the imagination of Boccioni, who had an almost mystical admiration for Michelangelo.

"Michelangelo!" he wrote in his youthful diaries (on the first of February 1908). "How can I dare use words to talk about him. Who am I? ... O, mysterious power of genius! I cannot follow him in everything. There is a point at which I see him cross a threshold and enter the Mystery. I worship him, that's all I can say! And it's even dear to me—and I don't know why—amid such an abyss of work and passion and pain and calm to think of him going in humility and sadness to the appointments the divine Vittoria Colonna made with him in the church which is up there on Monte Cavallo in Rome. What did Michelangelo say to the widow of the Marchese di Pescara? I know that she exhorted him to hope in God ... O infinite poetry of the world!"

The Casanovas may also have told their guest that this descendent of Vittoria Colonna was a painter of some talent, a watercolourist, and above all a great lover of gardens; that her husband, Leone Caetani, Prince of Teano, had been at the front for several months; that, even before that, the husband and wife saw little of each other, it being rumoured, in the drawing rooms of the villas and the gardens on the shores of the lake, that he was a surly character, an eccentric who didn't like socialising, and that she was a pleasant but nervous woman who was never still; and that their only son, Onorato, aroused a certain morbid curiosity, since he was a 'difficult' boy, who alternated between moments of uncontainable joy and bouts of deep sadness—his excessive height, his awkward movements and his halting speech pointing strongly to the possibility that he was mentally retarded.

Weather conditions during the first half of June were not ideal for painting. In a letter to a friend, Busoni complained about "a biblical storm" which, in the grandeur of that landscape, made him feel, he wrote, even more isolated. As for Boccioni, he would confess, in a letter sent to Busoni at the end of June, when the work had been completed, that "what with the terrible weather, the physical weakness [he] had felt at the beginning, and the twenty-four or twenty-six hours [he] had worked, the whole thing might well have been ruined."

The hours spent painting and talking beneath that curiously changeable sky, surrounded by mountains and immersed in the hazy light of the lake, soon became—to judge from both men's reminiscences—an intellectual refuge, an escape from the polite, somewhat predictable atmosphere of the villa and its rarefied, 'artistic' interiors. And those hours became even more agreeable to Boccioni once he realised, with relief, that the great Busoni was very pleased to be having his portrait painted. Far from being the impatient, domineering subject the artist had secretly dreaded, the maestro turned out to be a remarkable source of inspiration. Often, before posing, he would sit down at the piano and play a Bach sonata, or a piece by Liszt, to inspire both Boccioni and himself.

Boccioni would later confess to Busoni how afraid of failure he had been before starting. "Instead, everything was managed and controlled in a way that has never before been achieved in a full-length figure in the open air," he would write to him. "It's true that I had a wonderful ... unwavering model, and as I said your presence encouraged and excited me. My mind felt inflamed and alert. I am happy with my latest efforts on two of the small paintings, two landscapes and several things in the big one. In a few days I had gone through various stages and was well on my way to finding the right style. I needed to stay."

The portrait of Busoni—Umberto Boccioni's last important painting—is in the permanent collection of the Galleria d'Arte Moderna in Rome. It is an unlikely painting, which has surprised many Boccioni specialists with its apparent return to a kind of modern classicism, inspired by Cezanne. The seated figure of Busoni fills almost the entire canvas: a large one, measuring one metre sixty-six centimetres in height by one metre twenty in width. The figure is apparently static, absorbed into an equally immutable landscape of water, sky and mountains, and the lake in the background emphasises, by analogy, the atmosphere of stillness and contemplation. Yet we only have to look closely at the expression on Busoni's face and in his eyes and at the waves of pure colour in which everything—sky, skin, leaves, hands, water—is reflected and juxtaposed to feel the vital current that even today permeates the painting. In this work, the artist seems to have gone beyond dynamism as a mere mechanical element of perception and explored its deeper nature—the movement of thought or feeling. "We have to paint not what is visible," Boccioni had written in 1911, "but what until now was considered invisible, that is, what the clairvoyant painter sees." The 'motions of the mind'—defiance, pride, scorn, intelligence, humour—as captured by Boccioni's deep, sensitive eyes, can

Boccioni putting the finishing touches to his portrait of Ferruccio Busoni (standing next to him) on the terrace of Villa San Remigio (June 1916).

still be read on the face and in the whole figure of Ferruccio Busoni in the portrait.

Some photographs taken during those weeks at Villa San Remigio—probably by the Marchese di Casanova, who was an amateur photographer—show us the artist standing with his back to the camera, busy painting in the shade of an age-old oak. In the background, beyond the canvas on the easel, there is the vague presence of the lake and the mountains. Boccioni seems to be walking on tiptoe. He is wearing a straw hat, a light-coloured smock, tied at the waist like a kimono, and a pair of grey trousers. His body is leaning forward, towards the canvas, while the arms—the palate on the left one—seem to be vibrating horizontally in the air, as if marking the rhythm of a silent dance. Standing close to Boccioni in these photographs is Ferruccio Busoni, as imposing in real life as he is in the painting. He is wearing the hat that he holds in his left hand in the painting, and is leaning on one leg and smoking as he watches his young friend retouching the portrait.

What did the two men talk about during those hours spent working on the portrait in the open air? Busoni was not only a great student of Bach and Mozart but also a remarkably innovative composer and pianist, the theoretician of a new classicism in music—a style which looked to the future without severing its links with the past, which refused to renounce tonality until all its possibilities had been explored. Boccioni, too, was constantly in search of new expressive possibilities—in painting, in sculpture, and also in words.

Boccioni liked Busoni's Tuscan outspokenness, his passionately held opinions on modern art, his booming voice, the way he had of "always aiming straight and true in any discussion of aesthetic values". Busoni, for his part, admired Boccioni's rare combination of culture, intelligence, enthusiasm and humour. They talked about music, which Boccioni had loved from an early age. "I dream of giving my paintings the stimulating force of music," he had written a few years earlier in his diary. "To evoke through form the flights of the soul … "

Apart from investigating the boundaries between innovation and tradition in art, Boccioni and the composer discussed the war. Busoni was appalled and concerned by what he considered an obscure collective madness—"unbridled bestiality", he called it—which threatened to engulf the great European civilisation with which he identified. The young Boccioni, on the other hand, was a convinced interventionist. In Milan, in September 1914, he had been arrested for having, together with Marinetti and other Futurists, burnt the Austrian flag in the streets. Now, however, with all the projects he had under way and his magnificent Milanese studio at Porta Romana, so full of light and space, he would have liked to concentrate on art, not on war. By condemning him, paradoxically, to a period of mental inactivity, a soldier's life—of which he had had a taste the previous year, in all its boredom and harshness—felt increasingly like an imposition.

In his latest paintings, the Futurist Boccioni, perhaps influenced by Busoni's contemporary classicism and troubled by the growing savagery of the war, seems to have wanted to cling—even if only temporarily—to the certainties of the figurative tradition. The paintings produced during that final summer—apart from the portrait of Busoni, there were two small portraits of his wife Gerda and a few landscapes—seem a long way from the abstraction of his previous dynamisms, a long way, too, from the aggressive optimism of a year or two earlier. Things had changed. The war was drowning an entire generation in a tide of mud and blood. Gone was the immediate hope of a shining, optimistic, technologically advanced world (the great dream of the Futurists), and all that remained was the present, with its fragile, complex humanity.

On the morning of the sixth of June 1916, Vittoria Colonna Caetani, Princess of Teano, came ashore near Villa San Remigio in her little rowing boat. She had been invited to lunch by the Casanovas, who, knowing her love of art and music, wanted to introduce her to Ferruccio Busoni and Umberto Boccioni. The painter, for his part, must have been curious to meet the solitary inhabitant of the little island he had glimpsed from the belvedere. In addition, as someone who had lived in Rome for many years, he would have been aware of the significance of those historic surnames. Vittoria was descended on her father's side from one of the oldest feudal dynasties in Rome, the Colonnas. She had grown up in the family palace: a fortress built like a giant figure eight around two large courtyards, which contained—and still contains—one of the finest private art collections in the world.

"My father, my elder sister and I," wrote Vittoria in one of her books of memoirs, "lived in a beautiful sun-drenched apartment between the two courtyards, full of old paintings, which in Palazzo Colonna were as numerous as leaves in a forest during summer! The Colonna Gallery and the great hall … full of masterpieces, were on the floor below the one where we lived. As a child I loved to go down there during the long hot May and June afternoons. I would take a book with me and read, curled up on the marble floor, propped against the pedestal of one of the many Roman statues; often the book would close and I would sit there for a long time contemplating the pictures which recalled the glorious past of our house."

At the time she met Boccioni, Vittoria was only a few months short of her thirty-sixth birthday. Photographs taken during that summer show a woman with a soft, feminine body. Her dark hair is cut short, in a Parisian-style bob. The face, with its resolute features and large, melancholy chestnut eyes, is slightly elongated. The smile, although ironic and restrained, is appealing. Some dozen years before the war, during a reception at the Quirinale, she had caught the attention of the fifty-year-old King Edward VII, who had an eye for beautiful women.

He had asked her to sit with him and they had talked for a long time in English. The King was apparently so enchanted by young Vittoria's beauty and vitality that he had asked her for a photograph to take back with him to Buckingham Palace. Later, after her marriage to Leone, Vittoria would spend a few months every year in England, and the King would become a major figure in her life. Gabriele d'Annunzio was another fervent admirer of hers, as was the painter Boldini who, impressed by her aristocratic beauty, made a number of sketches of her, some of which were recently discovered in a notebook kept by a great niece of Vittoria's.

There was something proud and seemingly off-putting about Vittoria's beauty, but it was softened, and perhaps even enlivened, by the mixture of fragility, humour and restlessness that shone through her gestures and her words. In her adolescence, the princess had set a fun-loving tone for her young companions in Rome, organising daring games of bicycle polo in squares and courtyards. "One evening," she would write years later, "my father was taking me to a ball when he noticed a long, deep scratch on my cheek. I still remember how angry he became when I told him that it had been caused by the pedal of the bicycle of one of my companions in the game. But no amount of telling off could keep me depressed for very long."

Later, in London, her nickname was 'The Ballooning Princess' because she liked going up in a helium balloon. In the library on the first floor of the sixteenth-century Corsini palace in Rome, where the princess went to live with her son at the end of the war, her log book is preserved: a volume bound in dark leather with the words *Balloon Log Book* in gold lettering on the cover. Under the date of the second of October 1906, we read: "Most exciting trip. Dark night; wind increasing at times to hurricane. For some time travelled at the rate of seventy miles per hour. Lost all bearings, descended by the greatest luck within a hundred yards of the sea. Surprised at finding ourselves in Holland."*

* In English in the original.

On another of her balloon trips, Vittoria and her flying companions were overtaken by a violent storm which, as we read in a newspaper cutting preserved in the log book, kept them at the mercy of the wind and rain until well into the night. The flight ended with yet another forced landing and a few bruises.

At the time she met Umberto Boccioni, Vittoria Colonna had been married for fifteen years to Leone Caetani, Prince of Teano and eldest son of Duke Onorato and the English noblewoman Ada Bootle-Wilbraham, born on the twelfth of September 1869.

Leone—unusually for a Roman aristocrat—was both highly cultured and a great traveller. As a young boy, between the ages of thirteen and fifteen, he had written five adventure stories set in different countries of the world. The last of these was discovered in 2006, bound in green leather, in Vittoria's apartment in Palazzo Orsini. It was still there on the bookshelf where she had left it. Its title is *With Pure Courage: Adventures in Africa.* Its yellowed pages, covered in cramped, childish handwriting, tell a fantastic tale about a fifteen-year-old boy named Torre Ferraioli. Like Leone, Torre belongs to an old and noble Roman family. The author's vivid imagination catapults his hero, who is "bold and ready for anything", into mysterious, often wild places, a long way from Rome—a long way, too, from the sheltered spaces of a privileged childhood.

At the age of eighteen, as a gift for his coming of age, Leone asked his parents if he could travel to Sinai. This was no random choice. From his childhood, he had been attracted by the figure of his great-grandfather, the wealthy Polish prince Wenceslao Rzewuski, whose life was the stuff of legend and was recounted in the family with a mixture of curiosity and scorn. At the beginning of the nineteenth century, Rzewuski, as Leone himself would later do, had developed a fascination with Eastern languages and had learnt to speak, read and write Arabic. In Vienna, between 1809 and 1818, he financed the first orientalist review to have international contributors. One day, he left without any explanation and settled in the Syrian Desert, where he spent the rest of his short life like a Bedouin, raising thoroughbred horses. The one trace Leone's great-grandfather, the 'Emir' (as he was nicknamed by his descendants in the Caetani family), left behind him in Poland was, as Countess Rosalie Rzuweska, who was related to the Caetanis, recounts in her memoirs, "*Un immense jardin, devenu sauvage et tellement touffu qu'il semble être une forêt.*"* Leone, too, would leave a garden in Canada which is like a small forest.

Leone Caetani (as many letters written during his exile in Canada bear witness) liked to think that he had somehow inherited his Polish ancestor's temperament. A day would come when he would stop resisting that Slav nature which drove him to look for happiness in far-off places, at whatever cost. Imprisoned in a class and culture he found oppressive, Leone would feel increasingly isolated and marginalised, until he decided to leave Rome and his family history behind him. "There emerged," we read in a letter written to a female friend in the summer of 1921, "that Slav *insouciance* towards consequences and the future which has carried me along and emancipated me from many miseries and fears that keep other people in chains."

This tendency to shy away from the responsibilities of daily life, to take refuge in unfrequented places—the library on the top floor of Palazzo Caetani, the malaria-ridden countryside of the Pontine Plain, the deserts of North Africa and finally the woods of British Columbia—was a characteristic that ran through the whole of Leone Caetani's life, and also defined his relationship of mutual tolerance with Vittoria.

Travel, as he wrote at the age of eighteen in connection with the expedition to Sinai, was an attempt to "satisfy a certain

* "An immense garden, grown so wild and bushy that it seems like a forest."

Vittoria on one of her many ballooning expeditions in England (summer 1906).

vague, inexpressible restlessness which haunts my mind". That first experience with the nomads of the desert aroused in Leone "a strange, irresistible desire" to go beyond the boundaries with which he was familiar. His long youth (when he officially entered adulthood by marrying, he was already thirty-two) was marked by expeditions not only to the Maghreb but also to the mountains of Canada and to the Far East. Émile Zola, who met the twenty-five-year-old Leone at a reception in Rome in 1894, described him as "someone who has travelled, very large, very tall, and very naive." In his Roman diary, Zola also noted that, of all the possible mixtures he had encountered during his travels the most interesting was that of old Roman and Polish blood, and may well have been thinking of Leone when he wrote that this was certainly the "the best mixture", which had produced "artistic, if slightly mad, minds and spirits".

In the last decade of the nineteenth century, Leone Caetani, having put aside a degree in history and his studies on the papal court in the sixteenth and seventeenth centuries, set about teaching himself, first Persian, then Arabic. "How proud I feel of you, my boy, having conquered two such difficult languages,"* his mother wrote to him in 1888, when he was nineteen. Almost as a game, Leone began translating the twelve volumes of what at the time was the largest work of Arab history ever published: *The Complete History*, written in the thirteenth century by the historian Ibn al-Athir. This translation, which Leone would never finish, would constitute his point of access into the labyrinth of Islamic history.

In the first years of the twentieth century, after his marriage to Vittoria, Leone found refuge, as well as solitude and silence, in an absurdly ambitious project: to write the definitive work on the life of Muhammad and the origins of Islam. This work, claims the great orientalist Giorgio Levi della Vida in his biographical essay on Caetani, would have called into question almost everything previously accepted about the life

* In English in the original.

37

of Muhammad. Leone Caetani, writes Levi della Vida, was among the first in Italy to read the Koran in a political way, and among the first to explain the sudden, rapid Arab expansion in social and economic rather than religious terms. And it was Levi della Vida again—Leone Caetani's assistant on the *Annals of Islam* from 1911 onwards—who gave this description of the ambitious project: "To collect, sift and check an amount of material infinitely vaster than what has been left to us from ancient Greece and Rome; to supplement and illustrate it with data from countless auxiliary sources, often fragmentary, found throughout the vast range of religious, legal, geographical and poetic texts in Arabic; to compare it with information gathered from Syriac, Byzantine and even Chinese sources; to understand and translate it." An enterprise, he adds, "of such scope and such a major commitment as to demand of the person who undertakes it long years of intense preparation, determined and continuous effort, and ascetic self-sacrifice."

Leone Caetani, then, would devote the years of his marriage to investigating a distant past which did not interest Vittoria, and whose fascination she did not understand. To him, these studies represented another life—a parallel existence from which his wife was excluded.

The *Annals of Islam*, six thousand pages in ten thick volumes, are Leone Caetani's most mature (and most highly regarded) achievement as a scholar. Apart from analysing, through documentary evidence, the life of Muhammad and the history of the origins of the Islamic empire up until the fortieth year of the Hegira, the *Annals* offer a broad summary of the history of pre-Islamic Arabia. In accordance with Leone's wishes, the work, together with a valuable collection of old Arab and Persian manuscripts collected by Leone on his travels, now belongs to a foundation named after him, and occupies two book-lined rooms on the first floor of the eighteenth-century Palazzo Corsini, the headquarters of the Accademia dei Lincei, where, in spring and summer, the ripe, primordial scent of magnolia flowers wafts through the windows.

The Leone Caetani Foundation also houses papers relating to the prince's brief but intense political career. Having stood on behalf of the Constitutional Democratic Party in 1909, he was elected to the Italian Parliament, where he sat with the moderate reformist Left. In 1911, he shocked the aristocracy and the bourgeoisie by aligning himself with the radical Left, fighting long and hard against the annexation of Libya. He was accused of being an anti-nationalist, and subjected to a virulent smear campaign in the press. His reliability as a historian was called into question, and it was even claimed that the *Annals* were not his own work but that of his assistants. His political career—much to the disappointment of Vittoria, who had imagined his unstoppable rise to the position of 'first man in Italy'—was in ruins, as was his reputation. Having failed to win re-election in 1913, Leone Caetani withdrew from public life.

Despite their impressive bulk, the *Annals of Islam*—like many of Leone Caetani's enterprises—remain unfinished—a huge tree of paper and words which Leone's sudden departure for Canada cut off at the roots.

To judge from photographs, Leone was also a handsome man. Tall (one metre ninety-two) and slim, he had the athletic frame of someone who, from his childhood, had run and swum freely, aristocratic features, and the elegance of a man who had always lived among beautiful things, even though his eyes were often fixed elsewhere. Although many people, like his young assistant Levi della Vida, could not help noting in him "a certain coldness, which was not arrogance but which nevertheless created a kind of barrier between him and the world", others were not unaware of his sensual nature. He was an attentive reader of the *Kama Sutra* and since his youth had

had some complicated love affairs, often with more than one girl—or older woman—at the same time.

"He was a few years older than I was," Vittoria would recall, "and as he always lived in Cisterna, I had never met him."

She would meet him in the spring of 1901, amid the medieval ruins of Ninfa, at the foot of the Monti Lepini, in the middle of Caetani territory. The old town of Ninfa stands on the shores of a lake, and a river with unexpectedly cold waters runs through it. Its rich, dark soil is fed by springs which, as their water evaporates, transform the air of Ninfa into a soft, tangible substance. Despite the high walls which still surround it, Ninfa—with its seven churches, its hundreds of small houses, its workshops and tanneries—was destroyed in the course of one night in 1382, when the inhabitants of a nearby village, led by a Caetani, swept down from the mountain and set fire to their rival, killing most of the inhabitants in the space of a few hours. Over the next few centuries, Ninfa was to become completely deserted, helped in this process by malaria, until it became the "little dead town" so dear to the historian Gregorovius and other lovers of Romanticism, a place full of desolate enchantment, peopled by sinister legends. This grim but paradoxically irresistible isolation came to an end in the 1920s, when, after Leone's departure for Canada, his mother Ada Caetani and his brother Gelasio cleared the ruins of brambles and transformed the dead little town into a beautiful garden.

When Vittoria went there for the first time, the garden did not yet exist, and Ninfa was still a wild, mysterious place. At the time, Leone was spending part of the winter in the damp palace at Cisterna, from where the Caetani estates on the Pontine Plain were administered. When he was not riding about the area, checking on cattle and crops, he would write melancholy letters to his family. In the archives of Palazzo Caetani in Rome, there is a bundle of these letters, written to his mother during the last years of the nineteenth century on small sheets of pale yellow paper headed *Cisterna di Roma—Most Excellent House of Caetani—Campagna Office*. The handwriting is usually small, neat and round, but at times it shakes, as if trying to leap off the page. This was the result, Leone told his mother, of the quinine he took as a primitive anti-malaria remedy, and which had a bad effect on his nervous system.

In these letters Leone lingers over "the many difficulties with which [he has] to contend." Except when he was indisposed by fever, much of the time—he writes—he spent endlessly checking the accounts. In addition, he felt depressed. In a letter of the twenty-third of August 1898, Leone, in an unusual show of emotion, writes, "I feel so lonely and forgotten."* In another he complains about the gloomy palace at Cisterna, with its thick walls like those of a prison and its rooms which are cold and dark even in summer. In addition, Leone writes bitterly, there is not even a garden to walk in.

That day in April 1901, Vittoria had left Palazzo Colonna at dawn in the company of a group of friends. The automobiles in which they were travelling were among the first to inflict their roar on the city, bringing it a curious taste of modernity. The city, at that hour, was almost deserted, the bell towers and domes tinged with red, the sky clear, the air crisp. By the roadside, frost glittered like pearls of light on the grass and the dog-tooth violets. The party took the Appian Way, entering that vast territory that belonged to the Caetanis.

In the golden years of the *belle époque* before the First World War, the Caetanis were still in possession of their ancestral fiefdom, which fanned out from Lake Fogliano and the coast across the plain—thousands of hectares running alongside the sea, encompassing lakes and rivers and reaching as far as the Lepini Mountains, where the villages of Sermoneta, Bassiano and Cisterna are situated. "Theirs," Vittoria would write years later, "was more a little kingdom than a private estate."

* In English in the original.

A visible symbol of the wealth and power of the Caetanis was the myriad of mounted guards, who, as Vittoria recounts in her memoirs, were descended from the vassals who had served the family during the Middle Ages. Almost as though they were the cavalry of a tiny kingdom, these guards wore uniforms—jackets in the Caetani colours (sea blue and sun yellow)—rode wild-looking long-haired horses, used saddles known as *bardelle* (small caparisons) and held long sticks characteristic of the herdsmen of the Roman Campagna.

The Caetani motto, set in the family jewels, carved on the antique shields and the stone escutcheons over the portals of villas and castles, was *Non Confunditur*—No confusion—no mixing with others.

"We are not from Rome, we are from the Pontine Marshes!" Leone had declared one day, not without a certain pride, to Giorgio Levi della Vida. It was a way of saying that, through centuries of voluntary isolation within their own territory, the Caetanis had constructed for themselves what amounted to a world apart. "One might say that the Caetanis of the twentieth century," della Vida would write years later in his portrait of Leone, "still preserved something of the toughness and independence of a people who for a long time kept themselves aloof from 'the service of the wretched courts', and even, said those of their enemies who were more accustomed to the splendours and intrigues of courtly life, something of the toughness, simplicity and thrift of buffalo herders."

Vittoria was twenty when she met Leone Caetani. In Rome, she was considered one of the most enchanting girls of her generation. In England, too, she had many suitors. Her maternal grandmother, Leila Locke, after a disastrous marriage (her second) to the Neapolitan Luigi Caracciolo di San Teodoro—which had produced one daughter, Vittoria's mother Teresa—had moved to London. A few years later she had remarried,

Leone, Vittoria and their son Onorato during a holiday at Farnborough Hall, residence of the ex-Empress Eugénie Bonaparte, Vittoria's great aunt (c 1907).

her new husband being Lord Walsingham, owner of Merton Castle in Norfolk. It was there that Vittoria and her sister would spend the summers of their youth. In her last letter to Umberto Boccioni, the princess indulged in languid memories of those summers at Merton—memories, in particular of lost or unrequited loves. "I remember so well the rough feel of all those young men's jackets," wrote Vittoria, "you know that hairy fabric the English always wear in the country? They call it tweed and it has its own smell, of heathland and tobacco and I don't know what else, I would recognise it with my eyes closed. I wore short skirts for cycling, and my grandmother would tell me off because I was always laughing. Grandmother was terrible! She would tell me off for laughing, for coming back late on my bicycle, for flirting with the neighbours, for being happy, and for being eighteen. She told me off so much that I ended up crying, especially as I thought I was in love with an American who was in New York at that time and I had no intention of committing all those crimes."

Whatever feelings the young Princess Colonna may have harboured for the young American, they could never be realised. Her father, Prince Marcantonio Colonna, Duke of Marino and Assistant to the Papal Throne, was determined to arrange an important—and, above all, a Roman—marriage for his daughter.

The crucial meeting with Leone was not a chance occurrence—an uncle of Vittoria's had suggested that excursion into Caetani territory. Like many aristocratic Roman families at the beginning of the twentieth century, the Colonnas, despite owning property and land, were no longer as wealthy as they had been. A 'good marriage', therefore, was obligatory.

When Vittoria arrived in Ninfa, Leone—having escaped for a few hours from the narrowness of his life at Cisterna—was strolling in what remained of the *hortus conclusus*, a square plot of land surrounded by high medieval walls, chosen four centuries earlier by Francesco Caetani—governor of Milan, Viceroy of Sicily and grandee of Spain—as an ideal place for his collection of anemones. The *hortus conclusus*—where at the beginning of the twentieth century, apart from a kitchen garden maintained by the peasants and some beehives producing honey, there were still the remains of what had once been a grove of citrus trees—could be reached (and can still be reached) through a stone portal topped by the Caetani coat of arms with its stylised waves ascending and descending.

That morning, Vittoria crept up to the portal, attracted perhaps by the sound of water gushing in the ancient cisterns or by the smell of the vegetables and the first roses. Peering in, she spotted the man who, within a few weeks, was to become her husband. "I still see your dear face with your moustache *à la coup de vent** and it seems to me now that I loved you even then, although I know it's impossible!" she would write a few years later from London, recalling that first encounter. "Think what my life would be now if I had not gone through that gate."

That day, the meadows of Ninfa were covered in cyclamens and violets. The cold, clear waters of the Ninfeo river—in which even today, amid the clumps of watercress, rare speckled trout swim, brought back, according to legend, by Hannibal from Tunisia—flowed rapidly beneath the small bridges. Food, ceramic plates, glasses and cutlery with the Colonna coat of arms carved into the handles had been laid out on a linen tablecloth spread on the banks of the river. Leone was invited to join the group. The ivy-covered ruins, the thunderous noise of the water, the scent of the dog roses and wild jasmine, helped to create a "magical, enchanted" atmosphere which Vittoria would long remember. "In those days," she would write in her memoirs, "Ninfa was deserted and full of poetry." Leone's attraction to Vittoria was immediate. "We sat close to each other during the meal," she wrote, "and by the end of the day he had decided to marry me."

* in a windswept style.

Her father approved, and two weeks later Vittoria and Leone were officially engaged.

"I don't know what I've done to deserve such happiness," she wrote in her first passionate letter to her fiancé, in April 1901, "everything is smiling, everything is joy, it is enough that you still love me and do not discover *my faults*!"

The marriage between Leone Caetani, Prince of Teano, and Vittoria Colonna seemed like a match made in heaven. They were good-looking, cultured and multilingual, and shared a passion for automobiles and for adventurous travel. Despite their very Roman surnames, both of them, through their mothers, had strong cultural and family ties with England. They cultivated a taste for beautiful things, for gardens, and fine literature. They loved dogs.

The union of Leone and Vittoria did, however, cause a few raised eyebrows in Roman society. Within the old papal aristocracy, a small world of closely related families, this was the first Colonna-Caetani marriage in almost four hundred years. There was a long-standing enmity between the two houses that went back to 1297, the year in which Pope Boniface VIII (Benedetto Caetani) had excommunicated and exiled Cardinals Giacomo and Pietro Colonna ("that damned line"), accused of having declared his election to the papal throne invalid and of having led a strongly anti-papal party. He had also confiscated their property, dividing it between his own family and the Orsinis.

For centuries the descendants of Boniface VIII exercised absolute supremacy over the lands they had gained in the Pontine Plain. At the beginning of the twentieth century, the Caetanis were still rich landowners, partly due to the sound administration of the more recent generations and the support of the Savoys, who bought horses for their royal stables from Leone's British mother, the Duchess of Sermoneta.

The marriage of Leone and Vittoria in Palazzo Colonna on the twentieth of June 1901 was, therefore, a historic event that marked the reconciliation of two rival dynasties. For the occasion the throne room, with its great red canopy beneath which the Pope sat whenever he visited, was transformed into a chapel. "For once, the Pope's seat was transported elsewhere!" Vittoria would write. In accordance with tradition, the bride was presented with an old lace wedding veil. In fact, two veils: one which had been handed down by the ladies of the Caetani house, and one which had come to her through her mother, or rather from the Caracciolo di San Teodoros. Given that the marriages of her mother and her Caracciolo grandmother had been unhappy ones, Vittoria chose to wear only the Caetani veil: "in the hope it would bring me luck." Her long train was held by two pages, also dressed in white: Leone's youngest brother, Michelangelo Caetani, and Vittoria's little cousin, Piero Colonna.

"I was so happy, and it was such a wonderful day," the twenty-one-year-old Vittoria would recall in a letter sent to her husband on their first anniversary, one of the many they would spend apart. "And even though I was a little afraid, it's so nice to feel afraid of a person you love so much, it gives one more emotion, a delightful one!"

Prince Marcantonio Colonna had arranged for the wedding reception to take place in the baroque luxury of the Colonna Gallery, designed by Bernini on the pattern of the hall of mirrors in Versailles. Once the wedding ceremony was over, the representatives of all the great historic families of Rome, bathed in the golden light of the richly painted mirrors, paraded before the newly weds to pay tribute. Then, with much clicking of heels on the shiny marble floor and much swishing of silks and fabrics, the guests moved into the banqueting room in the seventeenth-century apartments of Maria Mancini, who, after loving the young Louis XIV, had married Duke Lorenzo Colonna.

Immediately after lunch, the Prince and Princess of Teano left on their honeymoon. Their first stop was a sixteenth-century villa in Frascati lent by friends, with a magnificent view of Rome, where they spent two weeks.

"And as it was then believed, with some reason, that you could not trust automobiles, which were in the capricious habit of always stopping half-way," Vittoria would recall years later in her memoirs, "we left in a victoria drawn by four horses, cheerfully waved on our way by the whole group of friends gathered in the great courtyard of Palazzo Colonna."

We have no way of knowing if Umberto Boccioni, who was nineteen at the time and had arrived in Rome just over a year earlier, read about the event in the newspapers. On the twentieth of June, for instance, the *Osservatore Romano* announced that the religious wedding would take place that morning at Palazzo Colonna. In the same announcement, we read that the civil wedding had taken place the previous evening on the Capitoline Hill and that it had been officiated over by Don Prospero Colonna, the bride's uncle as well as Mayor of Rome. The ceremony was "attended only by relatives: Don Marcantonio Colonna, Don Onorato Caetani, Princess Doria, the Count of Somaglia, Duchess Sforza Cesarini, her sister Colonna Chigi Zondadari, Countess Lovatelli, Don Livio Caetani, and the Princess of Sonnino."

To the penniless young man with a passion for painting, this list of aristocratic names must have seemed to belong to a very distant world, a world that clung irreparably to the past.

It was a past which would always be a major factor (if only as a model to be rejected) in the life choices of both Vittoria and Leone.

Vittoria Colonna was born in London one morning at the end of November 1880. Her mother, the Neapolitan Teresa Caracciolo di San Teodoro, was half-English. Her father,

Marcantonio, was the duke of Marino, and also, as Vittoria is clear to specify in her memoirs, "the first-born son of Prince Colonna of Rome". In other words, not just any Colonna, but a man destined from birth to both embody and add to the history of one of the oldest Roman dynasties. That was why, when Vittoria was born—another girl, after her elder sister Isabella—"the three generations that greeted [her] were really disappointed that [she] was not the long-awaited heir of the Colonnas."

When Vittoria was still a child (she was eight and her sister ten) the family was shaken by a scandal that caused a great stir in the small but ceremonious Roman court with links to the Vatican: the death of the twenty-seven-year-old Napoleone del Gallo di Roccagiovine, the nephew of Emperor Bonaparte, who had taken his own life, it was said, out of love for Teresa.

"According to rumour, which is always indiscreet and sometimes cruel," Paul Vasili writes in a gossipy but well-informed book on late nineteenth-century Roman society, "the prince was madly in love with the Duchess of Marino, the daughter of the Duke of Santa Teodora, who, the year before, had conducted a passionate correspondence with him but had then been cured of this passion by the admirable devotion of her husband Marc'Antonio Colonna. There are those who say that it was in fact the Duchess who rejected him for ever, while others maintain that the husband, although convinced that his wife had been faithful, had forbidden the unfortunate Roccagiovine to ever cross the threshold of Palazzo Colonna. The one thing known for certain is that the prince bequeathed to the duchess of Marino the tiepin he always wore—a sad memento of a poor butterfly struck to the heart."*

Contravening the golden rule which demanded that members of the grand aristocracy (especially those with links to the Vatican) maintain the public façade of a marriage, Vittoria's

* As Prospero Colonna pointed out to me, some of the aristocratic names mentioned in this extract are wrong.

parents separated. The two daughters remained in Palazzo Colonna under the distracted guardianship of their father and a long series of stern English governesses. Vittoria's profound emotional ambivalence can surely be partly explained by her parents' separation in such dramatic circumstances. All her life she would fluctuate between two apparently irreconcilable extremes: on the one hand, a desire for success and social recognition, on the other, an anxious longing for solitude. Following the scandal, her mother had to leave not only Palazzo Colonna but also Rome, and for a long time was only allowed to see her daughters for one week every year, sometimes a little more. "The first years were full of misery," Teresa would recall years later, referring to that traumatic family schism, "because the children were under their father's domination and I rarely saw them alone, but almost always in the presence of their governess."* For a long time, she was banished from Roman society and considered the equivalent of a fallen woman—not so much because she had had a lover, which was not uncommon at the time, but because she had abandoned him without being able to prevent the matter becoming public knowledge. In Rome, as Émile Zola notes in his cynical and amusing Roman diary, "if a woman breaks up with her lover she will be judged severely, whereas with adultery itself no judgements are expressed—the husband is of no importance."

The Roman custom of tolerating the impulses of the heart and of desire as long as they remained hidden behind an unblemished matrimonial façade may also help to explain the relationship between Vittoria and Leone Caetani. The initial *coup de foudre*—"It will be a great consolation for me to see a real love story in your marriage,"* Teresa wrote to her daughter a few days before the wedding—was followed by a few apparently happy months.

"Dearest mother," Leone wrote from Frascati two days after the wedding, "we are getting on splendidly and are so gay and happy that we believe nobody so happy as ourselves."

* In English in the original.

51

A few weeks later, he wrote from London: "Vittoria is very popular and well-dressed, looks charming and most striking—people turn round and look at her in the streets. We are very happy … "

Soon, however, relations between husband and wife became more complicated. Once the honeymoon was over—"for those two brief weeks," she would recall just over a year later, "we were perfectly alone for the only time since we became husband and wife"—and once they had taken their summer holidays in France and England, Vittoria lived through some very dispiriting times. Leone's repeated absences—every week he would spend four or five days at Cisterna, busy with the family estates—saddened her enormously: "Another day spent without you," she writes a few days before Christmas 1901. "I'm starting to feel like a sailor's wife … " A few weeks later: "I would like to have you here, my love, to kiss you really hard, to ask your forgiveness for all the trouble I cause you and to promise to be cheerful in the future and not to start again." In yet another letter, from February 1902: "I was very depressed when you left last night. I was hoping I could hide it but I don't think I really succeeded—by the time I fell asleep my pillow was quite damp!"

Within a few years, Vittoria had learnt to fill that void with frenetic activity. While Leone pursued solitude in the silence of the Pontine Plain or in the library on the top floor of Palazzo Caetani, she amused herself by taking painting lessons or throwing herself into the social whirl all over Europe. The two began to drift apart, but in an elegant manner, without arguments. When they did see each other, the encounters were often quite emotional: "I feel increasingly like your lover rather than your wife," she wrote to him in October 1907, "perhaps because the wedding ceremony means very little to me and I respect the bonds of love so much more." Moreover, from the first, Vittoria had been unable to conceal her annoyance at having to live in the cramped, austere surroundings of Palazzo

Vittoria Colonna and Leone Caetani in the gallery of Palazzo Colonna on the day of their wedding (20th June 1901).

Caetani, forced to share both space and Leone's affections with his family.

"When, during my engagement, I was taken for the first time to visit my husband's family," she wrote in her memoirs, "and I went in through the main entrance on Via delle Botteghe Oscure, my heart froze. A huge bearded grim-looking porter stood guard. I stumbled on the staircase and felt overwhelmed by the darkness. I implored my fiancé: 'Do we really have to live here? Couldn't we go to some other more cheerful house or even to a small apartment?'"

But this was impossible—in the Caetani house, as in many other aristocratic Roman houses, the rule was to obey the paterfamilias.

Very soon, the desert of those silences and those repeated separations was filled with an ocean of written words and small but reassuring domestic projects: apartments to refurbish, terraces to embellish, receptions and holidays to organise. Vittoria, to judge by her writings, was increasingly torn. On the one hand, she felt a growing desire for independence, perhaps inherited from her English mother and grandmother—or perhaps, simply, encouraged by the spirit of change that was sweeping across her generation: "You will find me a very different wife from the always languid and suffering one you have known until now," she wrote to Leone from London during the second year of their marriage. "Now I am full of an unstoppable energy, a will of iron, and a fiery character! … I *always* do what I want now, and if you try to stop me we will have a real battle on our hands!" On the other hand, she had an almost childlike attachment to her husband and son, and the need to make a comfortable family life for herself. "Because you understand," she would also write to Leone during one of her many prolonged stays in the English capital, "I love my independence, on condition though that I know I have a husband who loves me and a nest to which I can return!"

From the second year of their marriage, in any case, Vittoria spent much of the spring and summer in England. During the hectic London 'season', she became known, not only for her beauty and elegance, but also for her unbridled love of dancing. Cheerfully ignoring the admonitions of her father and husband ("Unhappy Tydy," she wrote to Leone, referring to herself, "who has simply gone from a stern father to an even more tyrannical husband"), Vittoria never missed a party.

"Would you like to know what time I went to bed last night?" she wrote to her husband on the twentieth of June 1903. "At 4.30 this morning, if you must know. It was already light, the little birds were singing in the square when I let myself into the house very quietly with my latchkeys and with my dress all torn, the tiara still standing, and my arms full of fantastic objects—cotillion gifts. Yes I confess, your wife, instead of staying in and sewing, had spent the whole night dancing … "

The hundreds of letters Vittoria wrote from London during the first decade of the twentieth century constitute a glittering portrait of the carefree, pleasure-loving life of Edward VII's court. The King would often invite her to intimate lunches, at which the best-known of his mistresses, the delightful Alice Keppel, was present, and would ask Vittoria to sit beside him and treat her to all manner of jokes and what she called his "belly laugh".

Vittoria came away from her first close encounter with Keppel in June 1903 with a mixture of admiration and envy. "It's curious to see the position the King's *chère amie* has. Everyone courts her!! She is a beautiful woman somewhat in the style of Maude Fortescue,* she makes a great impression and has splendid diamonds which she wears with immense brazenness, with wonderful gowns. Her income is eight

* A famous American beauty, and a cousin of President Theodore Roosevelt.

hundred a year! She spoke to me without any arrogance, very pleasant from the start, with a smile which is not without charm and a great facility with words. And today she left me her cards. God knows why she finds it worthwhile to pay attention to me!"

It was, in fact, Edward who was behind all this attention. Since first meeting Vittoria at the Quirinale at the beginning of 1903, he had taken a peculiarly tender interest in the young Roman princess. In June 1903, the twenty-two-year-old Vittoria appeared on the opening day of Ascot with "a *bleu ciel* dress, a new Paris hat" and (given that it looked as though it might rain) "a white parasol, and also a chiffon cape". This exquisite apparition proved irresistible to the King, who "was very pleasant", Vittoria told Leone, not without a certain smugness, "coming to talk to me, and after lunch he came to find me in the crowd and took me up to see the Queen, with whom I spoke for a while."

The following year, again at Ascot (a few days before being presented officially at court), the King invited her to have lunch with him and the Prince of Wales. This time, the Queen was not present, nor was the Princess of Wales. But Alice Keppel was there, along with what Vittoria ironically called "all the worst of that 'depraved society'."

Year after year, season after season, the encounters between the beautiful Roman noblewoman and the British monarch grew increasingly frequent—and increasingly intimate. "The King amused himself making me drink whisky which I had never tasted before," she wrote after yet another society occasion. "I found it disgusting and it ruined my lovely glass of Perrier for me." Naturally, the relationship aroused gossip. And although Queen Alexandra seems to have been taken with her, the King's mistress was clearly displeased. "Mrs K is cutting me cold," Vittoria wrote to Leone, "I think it's because the King talked to me for too long yesterday. She's furious when she thinks he's amused himself with someone else. I'm much more afraid of her than of him—because she could do me so much harm in London, that's why I'm acting with the greatest caution."

The King, however, did not desist, and, despite Vittoria's good intentions, there was a danger that the situation would get out of hand. Vittoria, who was eleven years younger than Mrs Keppel and a foreigner, feared reprisals. "I try to make myself smaller and to disappear where the King is concerned," she wrote to her husband, "because I'm so afraid of Mrs Keppel. She was much kinder to me last year perhaps because I had a scar on my nose, now she gives me dirty looks every now and again! They say she is ferocious towards younger women."

For a time, Vittoria beat a prudent retreat. But she would have her revenge—one evening in June 1909, during a dinner in London, the King insisted on her sitting next to him and "was not only very kind" to her but even—the wine he had drunk playing its part—whispered in her ear "that he had never seen [her] more *en beauté*." The following day the princess received a "hysterical message" from the wealthy Alfred de Rothschild who, at the express request of the King, begged her to leave immediately for a weekend at Halton House, his residence in Buckinghamshire, at which Edward, Mrs Keppel and the King's most intimate circle would be present.

Alfred, second son of Lionel de Rothschild, belonged to the English branch of the great banking dynasty. A tiny, frail-looking man, he was a cultivated aesthete, a dandy. As he had little interest in banking, he devoted his time and considerable amounts of his own money to furnishing his houses and acquiring paintings, being a great collector of works by eighteenth-century English and French artists. Halton House, cared for by Rothschild down to the smallest detail, was more than an aristocratic country residence, evoking rather the luxury of a maharaja's palace.

As soon as she received the invitation, Vittoria rushed to Hamley's, the famous toy store, where she bought a gift for Onorato, as a consolation for postponing the holiday by the sea she had long been promising him. Back home, she emptied her trunk of the "ordinary clothes" which she had made ready for the seaside and filled it "instead with very elegant things to appeal to Edward VII". Then she rushed to the station, where she found a private train waiting for her.

During that weekend, meals and entertainments—including a private circus with acrobats, horses and tame monkeys—alternated with brief strolls in the grounds. On these occasions, as Max Beerbohm recounts, the host, who was something of a hypochondriac, ordered his driver to slowly follow the group in the automobile (which appalled the sporty Vittoria) in case anyone fell ill. Several times, Vittoria occupied the "place of honour" next to the King, who was "very pleasant, even radiant". The forty-year-old Alice Keppel, who had previously shown such hostility to her young rival, was forced to capitulate. "Mrs Keppel," Vittoria writes to her husband with a certain satisfaction, "then came into my room to help me on with my dress and chat. We are great friends, she tells me to call her Alice, which means she is not jealous of me."

We do not know for certain whether or not Vittoria joined the already substantial list of the King's lovers. What is certain is that the attention shown her by Edward VII helped her to gain a prominent place in the very exclusive high society of London. In July 1909, the private view of an exhibition of Vittoria's paintings attracted a large crowd, and the King himself bought no less than five works. Photographs of her and articles about her began to appear in the society columns of the most fashionable newspapers—she was asked to write travel articles for various magazines, including *World* and the gossipy *Throne*, and she happily accepted. She took painting lessons, went on hunts, and attended performances in private houses. She was a friend of the Prince and Princess of Wales, the prime minister, Lord Asquith, who would give her affectionate if not very formal pinches at court balls, the Duke and Duchess of

Marlborough, Lord Vivien (with whom she danced and flirted, much to the annoyance of his wife) and the Londonderrys. The Duke of Connaught, too, often invited her to dance and, as Vittoria wrote, when he danced "he jumps a lot and turns very quickly", leaving her breathless. She also became a friend of the young Winston Churchill, who, when war came, would ask her for help in persuading the Italian government to enter the war on the side of the British.

After the death of Edward VII in May 1910, Vittoria and Mrs Keppel continued to see each other. "Yesterday I went to see Alice Keppel who has grey hair and the general air of being 'retired from business having amassed a considerable fortune',* as the newspapers would say," Vittoria wrote to her husband in June 1912. "I really like her house, and to me she is still one of the most amusing and pleasant women I know." United by a passion for furnishings, parties, and gambling, the former rivals became almost friends.

Up until the last moment of that golden era before the war, Vittoria continued to travel all over Europe in search of amusement. "My weakness for society," she called it. In the spring and summer, when she was not in London or on the French Riviera, she would spend weeks on end at the Villa d'Este in Cernobbio on Lake Como. To Leone, she wrote that when she was amusing herself—as she was during those days on the lake—she even forgot that she had a husband and son. "I made lots of people laugh the other day saying that if I received an offer of marriage I'd be quite capable, in my distraction, of accepting, so little do I have the feeling I'm married. Needless to say, a number of people immediately asked for my hand."

In those carefree years before war turned their existence upside down, all that mattered to Vittoria was to "amuse oneself and not to have to 'stop to think'". Hers was a conscious desire for escape: "I'm beginning to believe that happiness lies

---

*   In English in the original.

in not having time to think. When I think too much, I become depressed … "

What reasons did Vittoria have to be depressed? Certainly, her relationship with her parents had never been easy (in her letters to Leone, she often complained about how little affection the two of them had shown her). Then there were the tensions at Palazzo Caetani with her mother-in-law and sister-in-law, who, although perhaps not openly, blamed her for being a terrible wife. But what depressed her more than anything else was her failure to produce a second child.

"I try so hard not to think about it but that's not possible," she writes in June 1906. "For two nights now I've been sleeping badly because I've been hoping so hard, and today all my hopes have gone up in smoke … Fate is so cruel. Why deny me something which is so natural, such an honest desire? And then it grants it to poor girls who kill themselves out of despair! … "

Her letters to Leone in the years before the Great War and her meeting with Boccioni frequently betray a childlike need for love and reassurance: "I have had little affection in my life," she wrote. Once, perhaps in an attempt to attract her husband's attention, she admitted to him that she thought she would sooner or later end up taking her own life. At other times, she hoped that their only son would not also have to go through life with "*one skin too little* and feeling cold and pain in an excessive way."* When she was not out amusing herself, Vittoria would often spend sleepless nights smoking cigarettes, because, as someone who suffered from severe asthma attacks, she had the impression that they made her breathe more easily. This chequered life, in which social activity alternated with moments of deep solitude, caused her "a feverish anxiety" which she could only calm with veronal. Whenever she appeared in public, though, Vittoria was always perfectly turned out, the height of elegance, and many artists, like Edward VII's famous

---

* The italicised words were in English in the original.

protégé Mortimer Menpes, would have gone to any lengths to paint her portrait.

On the morning of the sixth of June 1916, when she went to meet "the Futurist Boccioni" at the Casanovas', the Princess of Teano—an amateur painter and a well-informed woman—was aware of his fame as an artist with an irreverent attitude to tradition. She knew that he was part of the Futurist group and that, like Gino Severini and Mario Sironi, he had been a pupil of Giacomo Balla. She knew of his international successes and the Futurists' travelling exhibitions. And she knew that, largely thanks to the poet Marinetti's flair for publicity, the Futurists had made a sensational entry into the realms of the leading European avant-gardes.

Among those whose interest had been aroused was Guillaume Apollinaire, who had met Umberto Boccioni and Gino Severini in Paris in November 1911. After having noted with a certain irritation that the young Italian artists wore "very comfortable English-style clothes" and that Severini was in the habit of wearing unmatched ankle socks—"the day I met him," he wrote, "he was wearing a strawberry-coloured ankle sock on his right foot and a bottle-green ankle sock on his left"—he asked them to explain their theories. As a theoretician of cubism, he was not at all convinced by the ideas of the Futurists, but he liked Boccioni. He was drawn to "that intrepid, loyal air", and was convinced that he was the intellectual leader of the movement.

During that first encounter at Villa San Remigio, what did Vittoria Colonna see in Boccioni, apart from a well-known, talented artist? In a letter to her husband, she speaks of his lively intelligence. It is a quality which shines through in the memories of many of those who knew him. "I still see him," the Futurist poet Paolo Buzzi would recall in 1924, "in that tight-fitting black jacket of his with the close little buttons and raised collar. His face with the profile of a blade, which was soon taken over by the cartoonists, had an incomparable mobility, luminosity and humour." Years after Boccioni's death, Marinetti would also evoke "that very elegant, refined young man" with a complex personality, who on the one hand "constantly revealed the melancholy of a dreamer and the tenderness of a man of feeling" and on the other "could also be the most impetuous and reliable of fighters."

With his dark eyes and hair, the "very Italian" expression of his face and "the agile body of an indomitable seducer", Boccioni charmed everyone. He had a number of "very complicated love affairs", his friend Severini would later recall. It was said that his lovers had included the art critic Margherita Sarfatti, later to become Mussolini's mistress. The longest-lasting of his affairs was with Ines, "the girl I first kissed" as he called her in his notebooks: a woman with a pleasant face, to judge by the paintings and drawings he made of her, and sad eyes. They met on a train between Trieste and Venice. She had a troubled family history: her father had vanished without a trace, and her mother had been forced to prostitute herself and her daughters. Ines had managed to extricate herself from that life, and now, even though she professed her love for Boccioni, was engaged to a well-to-do young man who could guarantee security. Her relationship with the artist was a turbulent one. "The illusion of love chills us," he wrote, desolately, after one of their encounters.

In some notes of his from 1911 he states: "The impossibility of being satisfied with half measures … the constant falling into extremes, the total inability to be satisfied, the furious desire to be loved, to forget myself, merging my personality with another whom I can feel mediate between me and the infinite: none of these things make it clear and simple for me to have a relationship with another person."

Nevertheless, the young artist was endowed with great vitality, and a remarkable sense of humour. "The divine gaiety of Boccioni," Marinetti would write. "The agility of his mind, which took bites out of all kinds of absurdities, like a young fox terrier with sharp teeth but without any spite." His laugh was unforgettable. "He could laugh to perfection with a cordial, intellectual, extremely communicative laugh," his friend Buzzi asserted. "And he showed those beautiful white teeth that reminded us of Poe's famous aphorism: 'Teeth are ideas.' But he could also concentrate, become absorbed, transform himself, and then his reactions would be ones of silence and ascetic composure."

This marked sense of ridicule and paradox contrasts with the deeply insecure and tormented character that appears in Boccioni's diaries and letters. "I have spent three days in hell," we read in one of his notebooks, under the date of the thirteenth of February 1908. "I hadn't been through such an anguished crisis for months. Everything had collapsed. The cause was everything. Art, life, everything! I increasingly feel the impossibility of living in contact with the world." In the summer of 1916—to judge from his letters to Vittoria—Boccioni was going through something similar. "I met you at a time of crisis in my methods, my friends, everything!" he wrote. When he wandered the streets of Milan, he told her, he felt overcome with disgust. "Everything seems banal and poor and pointless and vulgar."

It may very well have been this very mixture of humour and melancholy, vitality and despair, which attracted Vittoria, breaking through the wall of her light-headed, elegant solitude.

Of course, we should not rule out what might be called the attraction of the unknown. Her personal story was rooted in the almost thousand-year-old history of her aristocratic family. At a time before the war broke up the old social order

Vittoria at eighteen dressed as a nymph during a theatrical representation for charity in a private palace in Rome (1898).

for ever, the Roman princes still exerted the charm and power of a prestigious, separatist caste. The Roman aristocracy was so long established, and so intimately connected with the fortunes of the city and the Church, that it could be considered as being on a level with the great royal houses of Europe. The story of Umberto Boccioni, on the other hand, began and ended with him.

Their childhoods had been diametrically opposed. That of the young Princess Colonna, after her mother's departure, had been monotonous, marked by rigidly prescribed hours and duties. The only interruptions to the boredom of the long days in the palace, where Prince Colonna's daughters studied privately with their tutors, were lessons in dancing and horse riding. Every afternoon the duty governess would take Vittoria and her sister Isabella out in a large landau belonging to the Colonnas, drawn by two black horses, for a breath of fresh air at Villa Borghese or Villa Doria. The excursion would last exactly one hour. "Never a variation in the programme," Vittoria would write in her memoirs, "never a visit to monuments or works of art to show us the glories of our country."

During those same years when the Colonna sisters were being raised like hothouse flowers inside the ancestral palace, young Umberto was living through a restless childhood full of constant moves.

Boccioni was born in Reggio Calabria on the nineteenth of October 1882. Both his parents were originally from Emilia-Romagna. His father, Raffaele, was a local government clerk. His mother, Cecilia Forlani, the subject of many of her son's paintings and drawings, was a seamstress. Umberto also had a sister, Amelia, six years his senior. Their father's work forced the family to move often. The first great move took place just twenty days after Umberto's birth, when the

Boccionis transferred from Calabria to Forlì. By 1885 they were in Genoa, and a couple of years later they crossed the country once more, moving to Padua, where Umberto began elementary school.

In 1898, at the age of sixteen, the boy followed his father to Catania, Sicily. He attended a technical institute, worked as an apprentice at the *Gazzetta della Sera* and began writing a novel with the d'Annunzian title *Torments of the Soul*, which he would never finish. In November 1899 he moved to Rome, where he stayed with an aunt on his father's side who lived near Piazza Farnese. On the advice of his father—who in the meantime had abandoned his wife for a younger woman—he enrolled on a course for commercial artists. It was a profession he would come to hate, but, as he had no qualifications from secondary school, it would provide him with a living for a number of years. In 1900, during a musical evening at the Pincio, he met Gino Severini, who was then eighteen and had recently arrived in Rome from his native Cortona.

At the beginning of the century, while Vittoria was taking her first, difficult steps as a wife and mother in the gloom of Palazzo Caetani, Boccioni was frequenting Balla's studio in the Parioli district with his friend Severini. "He works day and night," he would later write of Balla, evoking those years. "He sees no one and visits no one. We disciples go and see him. He is always at work, alone, untouched by the world and its affections. He is pure and communicates his purity. He is serene and always hopeful. No word escapes him that is not an often ironic but always elevated observation. He is amazing."

Encouraged by Balla, Boccioni and Severini spent long hours painting and drawing in the open air. They attended the Free School of the Nude at the Accademia di Belle Arti, where they became friends with a neighbour of Balla's, the irascible, solitary Mario Sironi, who, after a serious nervous breakdown, had abandoned his engineering studies to devote himself to painting.

The twenty-year-old Boccioni's arrival in Rome came at a time of great ferment. A febrile desire for change was sweeping across Europe, and the younger generations seemed imbued with a hunger for renewal and a restless desire to smash the old hierarchies. In Europe, three royal assassinations took place in less than twenty years, all of them at the hands of anarchists or irredentists. The last of these assassinations, at Sarajevo in 1914, would lead directly to the First World War.

New artistic movements challenging academic traditions were flourishing in the capitals of Europe. Anything traditional, museum-oriented, 'antiquated', came to seem unbearable to artists who belonged, like Boccioni and his friends, to the burgeoning avant-gardes. Years later, Severini, recalling the Roman artistic establishment of the time, still mired, in his opinion, in a nineteenth-century aesthetic, would write: "Against such a background of vulgarity, banality and mediocrity, the stern figure of our Balla stood out. Following his example, and in reaction to such a background, my works and those of Umberto became ever more aggressive." In the rest of the country, he and his companions believed, "the atmosphere for painting at the time was the most noxious and harmful imaginable."

In the spring of 1906, the annual exhibition of the Amatori e Cultori di Roma rejected almost all of Boccioni's works, apart from one oil portrait and one pastel on paper, and all of Severini's. In disgust, the two friends put together in no time at all their own *salon des refusés*.

Two weeks later, Boccioni, who also claimed to be repelled by the artistic environment of Rome and could no longer bear his work as a commercial artist, left for Paris—"the brain of the world"—where he arrived on the first of April. In a long letter to his mother and sister, Umberto wrote that his life in Rome had embittered him to such a degree that, before leaving, he had seen only two ways out: alcohol or suicide. "I haven't been studying for two years because of those damned posters. They've ruined my nerves, I can't stand anyone any more, I don't love anything, I really feel ruined … "

This sense of youthful frustration did not last long, however. Boccioni was thrilled with Paris. "I am in a really extraordinary city. It's something tremendous, strange, wonderful!" Everything in that great metropolis appealed to his imagination and his craving for modernity: the trams, the automobiles, the Métro—"which is all lit up with electric light"—the publicity hoardings, the hundreds of bistros lining the streets. Finding himself "in the middle of these three million restless people running, laughing, doing business and what have you" filled him with optimism and a desire for action.

Paris also meant a kind of erotic reawakening. At the age of twenty-three, Umberto Boccioni discovered a new, and to his eyes irresistible, female aesthetic. It was not only a question of the many *cocottes*—"of those registered with the police there were eighty thousand!!!" he wrote with a mixture of astonishment and excitement—but even 'ordinary' women he brushed against in restaurants or cafés or walking in the street and observed down to the smallest detail: "I have seen women I would never have imagined existed! They are all painted: hair, eyelashes, eyes, cheeks, lips, ears, neck, shoulders, chest, hands and arms! But painted in such a wonderful, such a skilful, such a refined way that they become works of art. And this is true even of those in the lower classes. They are not painted as a substitute for nature, they are painted for pleasure, with vivid colours: hair with the most beautiful gold, and on it little hats that seem like songs: wonderful! Their faces pale, with the pallor of white porcelain; their cheeks slightly pink, their lips of pure carmine, finely and boldly drawn, their ears pink; their necks, the napes of their necks, their breasts very white. Their hands and arms painted in such a way that they all have very white hands, joined by very soft wrists to musical arms. *Taratantara taratantara taratantara!!!* You will laugh but I am in a state of constant pleasure."

(By way of contrast, Vittoria, who coincidentally was in Paris at the same time, commented that the "luxury of *toilette*" to which so many Parisian women aspired was really "exaggerated": "No one loves pretty things more than I," she wrote to Leone, "but the women here make it the study of their lives and talk of nothing else—the only aim of society is to have opportunities to put on new clothes—it's ridiculous!'")

Sexual customs were changing rapidly in that first decade of the century—women were taking their first difficult steps towards emancipation. And in Paris, all this was celebrated in the streets and squares, in fashion and in art. "It is a normal thing in Paris for girls to live alone," Boccioni wrote. "Almost all of them have lovers: the students, the seamstresses, the factory girls. Going to see a room, the proprietress of the hotel told me that she would give me one where there was a young seamstress, whose parents were in the provinces, but, she said with innocent casualness, the blessed girl has a lover and goes home every two or three weeks so that she can go to bed with him. And believe me, that's what many of them do. Just imagine, in a student demonstration on behalf of victims of the mines, the students marched in a column embracing very young girls, some of them were seamstresses. From time to time they would kiss … In the middle of them were female students dressed entirely in men's clothes. I was told that this is quite common at these demonstrations. People see all this and pass on."

The wind of freedom experienced by Boccioni was blowing not only through the streets, squares and universities but also through the drawing rooms frequented by Vittoria, who unfailingly described them to her husband: "From what I understand, all the women here, even the most placid and most respectable, have lovers." And they change them, she wrote, "as if they were hats."

In Paris, during that spring of 1906, Boccioni, who was then twenty-three, met Augusta Petrovna Popova, an attractive Russian woman a year his senior, who was married to Sergei Berdnicov, a Russian government official then on a foreign mission.

"As I told you," Boccioni wrote to his mother and his sister Amelia on the twenty-fourth of June 1906, "a beautiful young Russian lady took a great liking to me. Our friendship has become closer and the lady wants drawing lessons from me, for fifty francs a month." Augusta Petrovna was indeed beautiful, with her blonde hair and very light eyes, somewhere between green and blue-grey. She was also determined and passionate—it would not take long for their 'friendship' to change into a genuine love affair. That summer, Boccioni left for Russia with Augusta and her husband (it is not known if the latter was unaware of their affair, or simply indifferent). He stayed for nearly three months on the Popov estate at Tsaritsyn, where he was commissioned to paint a few portraits. By the time he left, Augusta was four months pregnant. Boccioni may well have been unaware—and would remain unaware—that the child was his. After Augusta's death in Russia in 1920, Boccioni's sister Amelia and her husband Guido Callegari would try, without success, to adopt the boy, whose name was Pietro. As an adult, Pietro had ambitions to become a painter and asked some of his father's friends, including Severini, for help. But he appears to have had neither talent nor luck. After the Second World War, in which he was a liaison officer in the French army, there is no further trace of him.

For Boccioni, the seven or eight years before the Great War were a whirl of new events and sensations. He travelled across Europe, to Paris, Munich and London, and dreamt of going to America. While continuing his complicated affair with Ines, he did not deny himself other adventures. In 1907, after returning from Russia, and after a brief interlude in Venice, he moved to Milan, where he worked tirelessly to support his elderly mother, who was now almost entirely dependent on him.

He was poor, but he had style. He soon became one of the outstanding figures in the group of young artists who gravitated around the Grubicy Gallery, which showcased the Divisionists, and in the cafés around the Accademia di Brera.

"He was wearing a Russian fur hat, knee-length boots, and a short overcoat with a large collar, also of fur," Luigi Russolo would write, remembering the first time he met him in Milan. "He could easily have been taken for a Russian. He had in fact recently come back from Russia and had visited a lot of the country, penetrating as far as the Kirghiz steppes! His clothes attracted attention, his eyes and his expression attracted sympathy. We introduced ourselves. Our ideas turned out to be similar, our artistic ideals very close."

His friends, apart from Russolo (who would later create the *intonarumori*, or noise machine), included the painter Carlo Carrà, a Piedmontese of anarchist sympathies, Severini—who in the meantime had moved to Paris—Carlo Erba (a Futurist painter and the scion of a well-known pharmaceutical dynasty) and the architect Antonio Sant'Elia. The twenty-seven-year-old Umberto charmed everyone with his sense of humour, his eloquence and his wit. "Boccioni thinks out loud," Russolo wrote in the same text. "It is a pleasure, a constant surprise to follow the rapid, lively, restless, tormented, brilliant flow of his constantly seething brain."

Boccioni's diaries of those years betray a constant tension. Despite his efforts, he was still unable to find an artistic language that was sufficiently free to satisfy him. He was searching desperately for a way to express in art the waves of emotion and sensation aroused in him by life itself, by contact with the world. "I have to confess that I search, search, search, but don't find. Will I ever find?" he wrote in a famous passage in March 1907. "Yesterday I was tired of the big city, today I long for it passionately. What will I want tomorrow?" He felt awkward, still too mired in the patterns of the past.

This sense of inadequacy, this anguished quest for a new language, was the driving force in Umberto Boccioni's artistic sensibility. When, arriving in Milan in August 1907, he went to see Giovanni Bellini's *Pietà* in the Brera, he was moved to tears—not so much because of the beauty of the work but because of its heart-rending restraint. "It is perfection itself," he wrote, "the effort of an artist who can go no further. There is everything in it. It is tremendous!!" This brings to mind the story Gino Severini told of their first day together, two budding artists busy drawing on the banks of the Tiber. Boccioni, who was not yet eighteen, sat down on a ruin almost surrounded by water and began to draw the Ponte Nomentano on a sheet of paper. Time passed, and Severini noticed with surprise that his friend's drawing had not progressed. "He had done it over and over again at least twenty times without ever managing to get the whole bridge onto the sheet," he would write years later. Boccioni, in fact, would start drawing the bridge at one end of the sheet and then lose himself in minute observation of every detail, every tiny shade, before realising, by the time he got to the other end, that he had drawn only half the bridge and that there was no more space for the rest. Subsequently, as he himself would write, he would learn "to rein in my eye for detail to the advantage of the whole". But the strength of his works also lies in this "infinite and laborious search", in the unresolved tension between form and desire, between the overwhelming nature of the sensations and the frustrating limitation of the means. "I feel empty, full of boredom, full of desires," he wrote on the fourth of September 1907. "Everything seems to me inferior to what I want. And I'm surrounded by the crudest vulgarity."

In Milan in February 1910, Umberto met Filippo Tommaso Marinetti, the controversial author of the first *Futurist Manifesto*, which had appeared a year earlier in Paris in the pages of *Le Figaro*. The week before this encounter, Marinetti had organised

Umberto Boccioni with the plaster cast of Synthesis of Human Dynamism (1912).

an evening of poetry at the Teatro Lirico, which Boccioni had attended as a spectator. The event had turned into a political demonstration, with the Futurist poets declaiming their pride and patriotism—a patriotism which, in their opinion, ought to lead Italy to declare war on Austria. The evening had ended with the arrest of Marinetti, among others.

The bond Boccioni established with Marinetti threw the doors of the new movement wide open to him, and it would be thanks to him, his talent and his hunger for the new that Futurist ideas would be adapted to the field of painting and the visual arts. During a night spent at the poet's house, Umberto— with the help of his friends Russolo and Carrà and Marinetti himself—drafted the *Technical Manifesto of Futurist Painting*, which would soon be printed on hundreds of leaflets and appear in the pages of *Poesia*, a review financed by Marinetti.

This manifesto, addressed to the "young artists of Italy", begins with a declaration of a community of ideals with the poets of Marinetti's circle. The Futurist painters, rejecting "the fanatical, reckless and snobbish religion of the past, fuelled by the deadly existence of museums", were opening the way to a new, transgressive sense of the beautiful. What they found beautiful, and worthy of attention, was, for example, "the frenetic activity of the capitals", "the very new psychology of nightlife" or "the febrile figures of the *viveur*, the *cocotte*, the *apache* and the alcoholic"—all of them figures who had impressed Boccioni during his first stay in Paris a few years earlier. The Futurist painters also declared themselves "certain of the radiant magnificence of the future". Phrases like these, imbued with a vitalistic and somewhat overheated optimism, can also be found in the letters which Boccioni sent Vittoria during the last summer of his life. "What I have to do has only just begun!" he wrote in a letter dated the twelfth of July 1916. "Everything is still to come and everything will be great and pure."

Two weeks after the drafting of the *Technical Manifesto of Futurist Painting*, Boccioni, together with the Futurist poets and painters, appeared at the Politeama Chiarella in Turin, where he would read the text to a very mixed audience—on one side, a crowd of young people curious to know about the movement, and on the other, those whom Marinetti called "about twenty mercenary rogues, sent by a coward I slapped in Milan". In the course of the evening, the readings were interrupted by the letting off of firecrackers, which were noisy but harmless. But then a fight broke out, from which the Futurists would emerge victorious, acclaimed by a delighted and jubilant crowd. This was the true beginning of the great Futurist adventure, with its scuffles, its proclamations, its laughter and its sleepless nights.

But the party was destined to be short-lived. The winds of war from Africa and the Balkans were beginning to ruffle the peace of the world. During the first months of 1912, while Boccioni was following the travelling Futurist exhibition, the Turkish-Italian war for the control of Libya was in progress. The Italians landed at Rhodes.

Boccioni returned to Paris in February, and stayed until April 1912 as the guest of Severini. Severini's studio was below that of Braque, who at the time was experimenting with lightweight sculptures made from paper, cardboard and other found materials. Boccioni visited artists' studios, galleries and collections, including that of Gertrude and Leo Stein. In April of that same year, he went to London with Marinetti for the exhibition of works by the Italian Futurist painters at the Sackville Gallery. At the time, the streets of London were overrun with thousands of women demonstrating noisily for their rights. Seized with enthusiasm (for the young women, rather than for their demands), Boccioni and Marinetti found themselves marching arm in arm with a "beautiful suffragette" (Marinetti's words) before the demonstration was broken up by mounted police.

Vittoria, too, in the years before the war, was increasingly caught up in the whirl of what she herself called a "disconnected and wandering" life. Since her son had left for school in Folkestone, England, in the spring of 1911, she had felt even more "homeless". Even the porters at Palazzo Caetani, when they were asked for news of her, or her address abroad, no longer knew what to reply. "As far as my return is concerned, my dear Ciù-Ciù, don't talk to me about it for the moment," she wrote to Leone from London in May of that year, a few months before the coronation of George V. "I was very unhappy to leave Rome but now I am under the spell of my dear London which has never seemed to me so seductive … there is a kind of *excitement* in the air and all sorts of beautiful things are expected."

But something was changing in their apparently static and peaceful marriage. For the first time in more than ten years, Leone wrote to Vittoria demanding that she return to Rome immediately. "I don't know why you're so insistent, seeing that I spend two months of every year in London and you've never before breathed a word of this," she replied curtly. The reason for his annoyance was that rumours were circulating in the drawing rooms of Rome that, during her last stay in Cap Martin, Vittoria had had a "desperate affair" with the son of some acquaintances of the Caetanis. "I'd like to put a bomb under that whole vulgar, boring Roman society, and start again from scratch," was Vittoria's angry retort to her husband. He replied that she should not worry too much, that "no questions will be asked",* provided she returned to the palace in Rome as soon as possible.

Vittoria therefore gave up on the celebrations for the coronation of George V, scheduled for that summer, and returned sadly to the fold. But by the autumn she was off on her travels again. And in February 1912, when Leone stood up in the Italian parliament to make his solitary, courageous speech against the annexation of Libya, as called for by Prime Minister Giolitti, she was not by his side. Many people in London praised

---

*   In English in the original.

the courage and wisdom of his position, but in Italy he became the target of a cruel smear campaign.

At the beginning of June 1912, a few months after the sinking of the *Titanic*, Vittoria again left Rome and moved to the Ritz Hotel in London, where she again began going out every night and staying up until the early hours of the morning. The Aga Khan, the spiritual leader of the Ismailis and a cosmopolitan bon vivant, said that he found it hard to believe that Vittoria's husband even existed, for the simple reason that in all these years he had never once met him. He courted her, sending her flowers and gifts and delighting her with parties which culminated in the spectacular, colourful arrival of Nijinsky's Ballets Russes, who were all the rage in the British capital at the time.

The other great amusement of the season, according to Vittoria, was the dances with animal names newly arrived from America: the bunny hug, the grizzly bear and the turkey trot. Her favourite was the bunny hug—as she explained to her husband, "Given that you dance very close to your partner and wiggle your bottom a lot, it isn't pretty but it has great qualities." With a touch of sarcasm, she added, "Shall we introduce it to Rome?"

On the eve of the war, however, it was in Paris, rather than in London, that the headlong current of modernity was most keenly felt. One day in June 1914, for example, as Vittoria was coming back from a picnic with friends in the forest of Fontainebleau, she was astonished to find herself caught up in "an endless procession of automobiles of all kinds". Meanwhile, she observed, "aeroplanes (at one point, three at the same time) and a balloon passed over our heads." She wrote to Leone that all this would have amused him because "one felt at the centre of civilisation". Within little more than a year, this vigorous, optimistic vision would be turned upside down, and these noisy human creations, bringers of speed and the kind of revolutionary technological beauty extolled by Boccioni and the Futurists, would bring death and destruction.

"Then our only troubles were personal ones," Vittoria would write in her memoirs, recalling the intoxication of those years leading up to the Great War, "and it seemed inconceivable that danger could ever come near us ... Our homes and our cities seemed as safe as the ground under our feet: we could not conceive our relations with people as anything but friendly. When we wished to travel we just bought our tickets, made our reservations, and started for any part of the world we fancied. Passports did not exist, and we changed our money unrestrictedly into any other currency we required. It now seems incredible."*

In Boccioni, the initial euphoria which followed Italy's dec-laration of war on Austria, and which would drive hundreds of thousands of Italians of all ages to join up, was transformed into a more complex feeling after that first winter spent on the front. By the time he arrived at Villa San Remigio at the beginning of June 1916, the artist knew perfectly well what he would find when he got back to the front: hunger, cold—a great deal of cold—and a frustrating lack of organisation and specific orders. The enthusiasm of the early days—"I am really happy," he had written to his brother-in-law Guido Callegari in 1915 in one of his very first letters from the front, "and you will see that Italy will rise to heights not even we could conceive"—had given way to a more opaque experience. He did not go back on his position, not even in his most private writings. But, as is revealed in his letters to both Busoni and Vittoria during that last summer, he had a strong sense of how much he was sacrificing in being forced to give up his art for an indefinite period.

For him, those tranquil weeks spent on Lake Maggiore, with no thought of anything except painting, beauty and purely sensual pleasures, were a time of extraordinary happiness and openness to life.

*   In English in the original.

On the seventh of June 1916, the day after meeting Vittoria Colonna at the Casanovas, Boccioni spent the morning painting (not for very long, however, as it soon began raining again) and talking to Ferruccio Busoni. After lunch, beautifully arranged by Marchesa Sofia Casanova, the perfect hostess, and coffee and conversation on the veranda, Boccioni asked to be excused for a few hours. He walked down through the intricacies of the garden to the little jetty on the shore of the lake, leapt into a little rowing boat and set off for the Isolino of San Giovanni.

Seen from the boat, the tiny, round island—no more than three hundred metres in diameter—was like a mysterious oasis, a shady garden resting on the water.

At that hour, Vittoria, followed by her dog Max, was no longer at work among the vases of flowers. She might have been reading or taking an afternoon nap, lying on the wicker sofa on the terrace—the one with the agaves planted in a row beneath the low perimeter wall, from where the whole of the lake could be seen against the background of Mount Mottarone. Or she might have been in the house and—as she always did when she saw a boat with friends or relatives on board—have rushed to the window, cheerfully waving her hands, and calling out directions to the landing stage.

Even today, the Isolino's harbour basin, a tiny bay surrounded by trees, can be reached through a small wrought-iron gate. On one side is a dense, rustling wood of bamboos, and on the other, on a promontory jutting into the water like an arm, is a grove of cypresses, which may actually have been planted by Vittoria. As he approached, Boccioni could not have helped but admire what remained of a "wonderful wisteria hanging over the harbour," whose flowers, Vittoria wrote to her husband, "are so beautiful against the background of the dark green water".

Having moored the little boat to the landing stage, he strode up the cool, damp flight of steps, lined even today by a tangled little wood of palms, redwoods and cypresses. At the top of the steps, on the left, was the villa, a former seventeenth-century monastery flanked by a chapel with a slightly convex façade topped by a slender iron cross.

Vittoria was there waiting for him.

"I feel a great attraction towards the forms of an elegant life," Boccioni had written ingenuously years earlier, at the age of twenty-four. "For me, everything is elegant when I find that harmony of line that fires my imagination just like musical notes."

What did Umberto Boccioni's inquisitive eyes see during that first visit to the island?

For two years, ever since she had rented it from the Borromeos in the autumn of 1914, Vittoria Colonna had devoted herself to transforming the little island into a temple to beauty, the care of nature and the small pleasures of life—flowers, reading, strolls, short swims in the lake, hours devoted entirely to embroidery (a passion the princess would nurture throughout her life), work in the kitchen garden, and good conversation—pleasures which seemed even more sweetly fleeting than ever during those war years.

The Isolino, with its freshly painted house, its comfortable wicker sofas placed here and there in the shade of the pergolas, and the thick clouds of tiny pink roses (in early June, the wonderful Dorothy Perkins roses, planted by Vittoria, were in full bloom), was extremely elegant. "I've tried to combine the comfort which England has taught us," she had written the year before to her husband concerning her work on the Isolino, "with the picturesque Italian character." In the drawing room, which Vittoria showed Boccioni that day, the walls had just been painted white, like the rest of the house. The curtains and the fabrics on the sofas "were of thick turquoise blue canvas, the colour of the lake which can be seen from the large window". She had chosen them for their "fresh, lively effect"—so different from the interiors, laden with history and objects, in which she had always lived. And a long way, too, it would seem, from the horrors of the front, as reported every day in the newspapers. "In my little house fresh air circulates from all sides and there is a great sense of calm—all you can hear is the soft sound of the waves of the lake on the rocks beneath the window. It seems impossible that there is a war on!"

Umberto Boccioni may also have noticed the framed photograph of Leone Caetani in the drawing room. Now that her husband was away at the front, Vittoria had propped it in a conspicuous position on a small table, and had surrounded it with small vases full of fresh flowers from the garden: "like a little altar", she had written to Leone.

And surrounding the house, Boccioni may have noticed the signs that there was a great deal of gardening going on. The clearing opposite the front of the house had been marked out by her with boxwood hedges which, although still tiny and delicate, already created elaborate patterns which would eventually evoke the grace of an eighteenth-century garden. In the days that followed, Boccioni—with ironic high-handedness—would dub it the Garden of Victory.* Here and there, roses and jasmines crept over the columns of the pergolas and the old, plastered walls of the church, in which were two small ducks which Vittoria and the governess Gertie were lovingly tending. "To think that we are taking so much trouble to keep two little animals alive," Vittoria wrote to Leone, "while all over Europe men are doing all they can to kill each other!" There was also a pigeon house with baby pigeons. In the shade of the camphors and magnolias, Boccioni is also likely to have admired the huge hydrangea bushes with their big white and blue flowers, of which Vittoria was particularly proud.

---

*   In Italian, 'Il Giardino della Vittoria', the name Boccioni gave the garden, could mean both 'the Garden of Victory' and 'Vittoria's Garden'. (Translator's note)

That afternoon, Vittoria Colonna and Umberto Boccioni sat down on the terrace to take five o'clock tea. It was an elaborate daily ritual, accompanied by home-made cakes and biscuits, which Vittoria would never willingly forgo. Then they went for a long walk, which would certainly have lasted until what she called "the most beautiful time" on the Isolino—sunset. Vittoria may have enjoyed herself taking her new friend to discover the secret places of her island: the terrace with the English roses; the 'retreat' directly above the lake with its stone bench surrounded by ivy; the small eighteenth-century altar of white and blue ceramics depicting the good shepherd, hidden amid foliage not far from the harbour basin. Vittoria, always absorbed in her little projects, would have pointed out to Boccioni the hen house she was planning to build. She may also have shown him the avenues paved the previous year with large flat stones collected on the beach, as well as the bowling green which her son Onorato was in the middle of laying out at the bottom of the garden with the help of Gertie's handyman husband Italo. Then they may have gone down the paved path and through a little iron gate, and even further down as far as the Isolino's little beach of damp, thickly packed sand, one of Vittoria's favourite places, not only for the clear water into which she loved to plunge—even though she had never learnt to swim very well—but also, and above all, for the wild beauty of its vegetation.

"On one side of the island," she had written the previous year to her husband, "there is a tiny beach, with trees that grow with their roots in the water, the roots are red and in the grass I found forget-me-nots. I will sow some more so that approaching from that side you will be gently greeted by those little flowers."

Today, between the cracks in the immense stone wall that supports the ground behind the beach, a huge prickly pear has emerged. In the spring, looking here and there under the oleander bushes and along the path which leads from the beach up to the villa, it is still possible to glimpse the dazzling blue of the forget-me-nots. In all probability, they are the descendants of those first sowed by Vittoria during the winter of 1915.

How did Vittoria Colonna Caetani, a Roman princess, come to be living alone (apart from her fourteen-year-old son and a few servants) for several months of the year on a little island so close to the front? Whenever she was asked, Vittoria would reply that it had been by chance—an unexpected gift which life had given her in September 1914.

By 1914, Vittoria's father Marcantonio Colonna had been dead for a few years and his widow Teresa Caracciolo—who, following the famous scandal so many years earlier, had never been reconciled with him—had inherited a large sum of money which allowed her, among other things, to rent Villa Maria at Pallanza on Lake Maggiore (it would become her favourite place, and she would be buried there). Teresa needed peace and quiet. For years she had been suffering from mood swings, with long months of depression alternating with phases of uncontrollable, maniacal excitement. During these latter phases, Teresa (who was still a beautiful woman at the age of fifty-nine) would be unable to sleep, would gamble away incredible sums, and would fall madly in love with anyone who paid her a little attention. At such times—as Vittoria and her sister Isabella well knew—she had to be watched closely and calmed with massive doses of bromide: "She's always very original," Vittoria wrote to Leone from the Ritz in London in 1912, during a particularly euphoric phase of her mother's, "strangers don't realise it, but living with her I am struck by her total inability to think clearly—and her excitability! All she thinks about is men and marriage, I feel like an old matron who has to chaperone her!!"

When Vittoria went to see her mother at the beginning of September 1914, the conflict was increasing. "The situation

Vittoria on the Isolino (summer 1916).

increasingly resembles a dogfight," Vittoria had written to Leone on the fifteenth of August that year, "with new, rabid little dogs entering the mix." Teresa was still in her manic phase, but all things considered was well. She seemed in a good mood. Mother and daughter spent the days going on excursions and making social visits. They went for walks on Mount Mottarone, visited Lake Orta and the Borromean islands on Lake Maggiore, and ate fresh fish in a small but highly regarded restaurant on Isola dei Pescatori.

Among the many beauties of the lake, however, it was the Isolino di San Giovanni which most captivated Vittoria.

"I won't hide from you the fact that I am entertaining a golden dream, which is so beautiful that I do not dare think about it too much," she wrote to Leone on the twelfth of September 1914, adding that she did not dare reveal to him the object of her dream. In the same letter, after various tangents, she finally confessed: "I can't bear it any more: I have to tell you what I'm talking about. It's the Isolino … Darling, darling! Just *think*,* a little green island in the middle of a blue lake, or rather not in the middle; so far to one side that it takes only twenty or thirty *seconds* by boat to reach the other shore. A little island that would be all mine, a little kingdom! And at the top of it, a white house, in which the best room would be for you, with a wonderful view of the water and the mountains. And a garden, too, with cypresses and boxwood hedges—just think! I would work in it all day. And when you're cold we'll make you a nest in the sun, and when you're hot we'll make you a den in the shade, and by day you would go for walks in the mountains … But it's so beautiful that I don't want to think about it, because I want it too much, and life lately has been giving me nothing but disappointments … "

The Isolino, then, immediately assumed in Vittoria's eyes the unreal contours of a happiness she had often imagined and never attained. She had found, she wrote, "the little house and

* Vittoria underlines this word twice.

garden of [her] dreams" and this could finally cure her once and for all—she implied to Leone—not only of the "melancholy" and the "dark moods" that had been plaguing her for some time but also of her unquenchable desire for escape.

The situation of the Isolino di San Giovanni, however, was unclear. For many years it had been rented on a regular basis by Count Metternich, the former German ambassador to London, who, now that the flaming circle of hostilities was widening, was anxious to leave Italy as soon as possible before she declared war on his own country. The Isolino seemed to be available—until Vittoria learnt that a German lady, a friend of Metternich's, wanted to take over the island for herself.

"Sad! Sad!" wrote Vittoria, desolately, to her husband on the thirteenth of September 1914. "I've never wanted anything more than I want this little island … "

Vittoria therefore asked Metternich to support her, and during the exasperating wait spent her days on the island. "I have continued to explore it," she wrote to Leone, "always discovering new beauties—I no longer dare think about it." And again, the next day: "The Isolino has become an obsession. I have written to Metternich but unfortunately I don't think there is any hope. And I am ever more in love with it. I go there every morning, I examine all of it, I already have countless plans in my head—but I try not to think about it because I feel it's pointless. It would be *too* beautiful."

At last, when she had almost given up hope, the long-awaited news arrived. The German lady had withdrawn, scared off by the war. In a letter written at Villa Maria on the seventeenth of September, Vittoria announced triumphantly to Leone: "My darling, Metternich has telegraphed that I can have the Isolino if I can come to an agreement with the Borromeos!!"

The rent, she added, would be five thousand lire a year; but her mother, happy to have Vittoria with her during the summer months, promised to pay two-thirds. That was not all—Teresa, who was evidently going through a phase of euphoric generosity, also insisted on giving her daughter enough money to restore both the house and the garden. Vittoria was delighted, but Leone did not share her enthusiasm. He could not understand why his wife, who already spent so many months of the year away from him and Rome, had got it into her head—with all the properties owned by the Caetanis—to rent an entire island on a lake many hundreds of kilometres from home.

But for Vittoria, what made the prospect so attractive was precisely the distance separating the Isolino—which from now on she would call "my private kingdom"—from Rome and the "grim Palazzo Caetani" where she had been forced to live since her marriage.

Like many Roman palaces, Palazzo Caetani was more reminiscent of a small fortress than a family residence. Its construction was typical of the sixteenth century: a symmetrical façade, large rectangular windows with stone frames and ledges, also in stone, in the shape of small waves. An imposing central doorway above which the name Caetani was carved in large Roman characters, led into a dark marble courtyard. There was no garden. Compared with other palaces, like those of the Colonnas, the Doria Pamphilis, or the Odescalchis, it was less refined, but conveyed—and still conveys today—a strong sense of power.

"It is impossible to imagine," Vittoria wrote in her memoirs, "two abodes more utterly different than my old home, Palazzo Colonna—so spacious, so full of light and sunshine, with its wonderful old gardens and enormous courtyards, its priceless picture gallery and innumerable frescoed walls—and Palazzo Caetani, in Via delle Botteghe Oscure, the street of the dark shops, one of the narrowest streets in Rome.'*

---

*   This is no longer the case—today it is a broad sunlit street which joins Largo Argentina to Piazza Venezia. This quotation is in English in the original.

At the beginning of the twentieth century, when Vittoria became a member of it, the Caetani family consisted of Vittoria's parents-in-law, the Duke and Duchess of Sermoneta, and their six children. For each of them, starting with the firstborn, Leone, an unusual and recognisably Caetani name had been chosen at birth—Giovannella, Roffredo, Livio, Gelasio, Michelangelo—names that marked out a mental territory and signalled the fact that they belonged to a line which, even after nine centuries, still held a dominant position in the Roman world, or rather, the Italian world, since Rome had become the capital of Italy in 1870.

The young Caetanis were all tall and good-looking, and in the best Anglo-Saxon tradition—resolutely followed by the English-born Duchess of Sermoneta—each of them cultivated a particular talent. Giovannella and Livio both wrote, Roffredo played the piano and composed music, while Leone and Gelasio studied to great advantage. The youngest, Michelangelo, being weak and sickly, was excused the obligation to excel. From their earliest youth, the Caetanis were encouraged to read, to travel, and to display their interests. "Take as many music lessons as you like," was the Duke's exhortation to the adolescent Leone—he would learn to play the piano and the pianola.

The Caetanis got on well with one another, which was why they found it the happiest, most natural thing in the world to all live together, even as adults, in the same palace. Vittoria found this incomprehensible, and would often declare that she hated the very idea of family: "I abhor relatives in general." And, talking about Leone's brother, whom she saw sometimes in Paris, she would add: "I like Gelasio *despite* the fact that he's my brother-in-law." As soon as she set foot in Palazzo Caetani, therefore, Vittoria, accustomed to the marmoreal silences of the huge Palazzo Colonna, immediately began to complain about the overcrowding and the prevailing disorder.

"None of the family had any idea of time or tidiness," she wrote in her memoirs, "and the palace was in a chronic state of confusion and dust. From the day I entered it until the day I left I always saw workmen going about the place carrying saws, hammers, and pots of paint; huge ladders were dragged up and down stairs by perspiring underlings, and loud shouting of directions, chiefly from the upper windows down to the courtyard, went on most of the day. But there was never any perceptible result; the dirt and disorder remained always the same and the family, far from being discouraged, regarding this state of things as a standing joke."*

What Vittoria found most difficult to bear was the complete lack of privacy. Not only were she and Leone expected, at least in the early years, to share the table at lunch and dinner with his parents, his brothers and his sister (who, after the premature death of her husband, the Belgian Baron Grenier, had come back to live in the family home with her young children), but it was also understood that they would share whatever belonged to them with the rest of the family. At one point, Vittoria's parents-in-law decided that some pieces of furniture that had come from Palazzo Colonna would go very nicely in their villa at Fogliano, which had recently been restored. From London, Vittoria forbade Leone to take a single one of her belongings. And she declared that "the system of shared property" so dear to the Caetanis was not for her. "It gets on my nerves," she declared. "The coach isn't mine, the cook isn't mine, my servants are overworked by everybody, but at least I want to keep my furniture—I may not need it now, but I will certainly need it later!"

Even her sense of order and punctuality, instilled in her by a particularly strict upbringing, was strained to the limit by the Caetanis: "None of my family-in-law ever dressed for dinner and during that first winter, when we lived all together, I think I sat longer at the dining-room table than I ever have since in my life. A bell rang before meals to summon us all, but no one ever

* In English in the original.

dreamt of moving towards the dining room or hearing it, for the Caetanis merely considered it as a symptom that food might be expected before too long. The story ran that the duchess always said on hearing the luncheon bell: 'That's nice, I still have time to go to the stables and see all the horses.'"*

The Caetanis expressed their irrepressible individualism even at table, where each person's tastes were sacred. When Vittoria, in the early years of her marriage, sat down to lunch with the family (subsequently she would manage to persuade her husband to have their meals, whenever possible, in the apartment which had been assigned to them on the second floor of the palace), she was surprised to find a myriad of containers on the table filled with various sauces, salted sardines, and food in oil and vinegar. "Each person's place at table," we read in her memoirs, "was distinguished by a group of little cans and boxes belonging to that person."

Another thing that Vittoria found strange was that, in spite of their great wealth, the Caetanis were extremely mean. At the beginning of the eighteenth century, the family, who up until then had mostly lived on their estates in the Pontine marshes, aloof from the spendthrift, pleasure-loving ways of Roman high society, moved to Rome for good. Their expenses—balls, coaches, clothes and servants—increased to an astronomical extent.

"Whether rich or poor," wrote the Frenchman Edmond About in a volume on Rome published in 1861, "a Roman prince is expected to maintain a style of life commensurate with his rank, because his prime duty is to keep up appearances. It is therefore necessary for the façade of the palace to be repaired, for the reception rooms to be very luxurious, for the gallery not to arouse the pity of foreigners by the state of neglect in which it is left. It is necessary for there to be many servants, for the servants' livery to have plenty of braid, for the coaches to be newly painted, and the horses well fed, even if it means the masters doing without one course at lunch. It is necessary for

* In English in the original.

the dependants of the house to be helped when in need, and for the beggars to bless the lord's generosity. It is necessary for the clothes of the lord and lady to be not only elegant but also rich—since, ultimately, the nobility must not be confused with the middle classes. Last but not least, it is necessary for a boring but sumptuous party to be given once a year which will consume in candles a quarter of the income for the entire year. If anyone failed in one of these obligations, he would fall into the ranks of the faded lords who hide away and prefer to be forgotten."

By the beginning of the nineteenth century, despite their vast estates, the Caetanis were on the verge of bankruptcy. It was Duke Michelangelo, Leone's grandfather and a man of great culture, who managed, with good humour and much sacrifice, to turn around the family's shaky finances. According to an article that appeared in the *Corriere della Sera* in 1892, the Duke paid off his debts, increased the family income, put everything into scrupulous order, and for nearly forty years practised the strictest economy.

Having caught a whiff of the acrid smell of poverty—a relative poverty, but one that would have been sufficient to topple the Caetanis from the Olympus of Roman power—Michelangelo turned stinginess into a fine art. "Clever, witty, artistic and extra economical": these were the adjectives used by Mrs Paget, the wife of an English ambassador to Rome, to describe the old Duke of Sermoneta in her memoirs.

While other families of more recent nobility, eager to assert themselves or to remain at the summit of court life, threw themselves into a lavish lifestyle, heedless of the expense, the Caetanis—strengthened by their ancient roots—lived with a moderation that verged on the eccentric.

Duke Michelangelo preferred to walk everywhere rather than take his coach. For a time, he rented out his apartment on the *piano nobile* and adapted himself to living with extreme sobriety in small rooms on the mezzanine which he called "the catacombs" or "the hermitage of the Botteghe Oscure" because of the lack of light. In addition, Don Michelangelo had very simple tastes. He often dined in taverns on plain food such as fettuccine, kidneys, fried fish, ricotta, and large plates of wild chicory. He hated French cuisine and palace cooks. It was said that once, when a foreign traveller asked permission to visit some of his properties in the Pontine marshes, including the castle of Sermoneta, he replied: "I would even gladly invite you to lunch but I should tell you that, unfortunately, my cook died … at the end of the sixteenth century."

"Duke Michelangelo," we read in Vittoria's memoirs, "was a witty man. It is said that he travelled third class—something unheard of at the time for a gentleman—and when asked why, replied, 'Because there isn't a fourth class.'"

Leone would subsequently demonstrate that he had inherited his ancestor's stoical contempt for what he considered needless comfort. In the first years of his voluntary exile in Canada, for example, the only luxury he allowed himself were books and magazines which he had sent to him regularly from Italy and England. Then he gave these up, too. His life with his new family in the town of Vernon would be marked by total simplicity. Leone would learn to cook, to cut wood in the forest both to sell and for heating, to do the washing and to keep his little house clean: "Anything not to have servants and dependants!" he wrote to a friend in 1921.

Vittoria was quite different. During one of her first shopping expeditions to London as a married woman, she announced triumphantly to Leone: "Yes, I have become very spendthrift and I advise you to have a novena started in church immediately. I have bought more hats … The money flies away in a rain of gold wherever I go. Cabs will end up ruining me for good, but what can I do?"

It is not hard to see why Vittoria (who also liked gambling at poker and bridge) soon became unpopular with the Caetanis.

They could not tolerate what they interpreted as a brazen desire for independence, and they deplored her long, costly journeys without her husband. For her part, Teresa Caracciolo never lost an opportunity to ridicule her in-laws' meanness. One day in London, sitting down to a meal after yet another morning spent shopping, Teresa remarked that she had heard from everyone that "the Caetanis are extraordinarily stingy, and that it's a real illness".

In addition, from the earliest years of her marriage, it was rumoured, and not only at Palazzo Caetani, that, just like her mother, the restless Vittoria could not resist the temptation to take a lover from time to time. "Who is it who speaks ill of me?" Vittoria asked her husband in a letter. "I assume the first floor [where her parents-in-law and her sister-in-law Giovannella Caetani Grenier lived] has something to do with it."

These were mere shadows, however, annoying certainly, but which Vittoria Colonna managed to dismiss with a gesture of her beautiful hand—or by leaving Rome on some new pretext. What, on the other hand, did throw a genuinely dark shadow over her life, and arouse genuine anguish, was her son Onorato.

It had been a painful pregnancy, followed by a difficult labour, but, although born underweight, the child, with his big dark eyes and head covered in brown curls, was in good health. Up until the age of four or five, Onorato does not seem to have shown any particular difficulties, even though—despite the constant presence of a tutor—he spoke little and when he became excited would stammer incomprehensibly. "He is rather nervous and very strong-willed," Leone would write to his mother when his son was five, "though at times he seems so quiet and meek. One must be very careful how to handle him."*

One of the first references to Onorato's "strangeness" comes in a letter Vittoria wrote to her husband at the end of September 1907. At the time she was with her mother on Lake

---

* In English in the original.

Como, where she had gone to paint. Leone and Onorato were at Balcarres in Scotland, on the estate of Leone's maternal aunt. In the course of the days he spent with his son—a rare occurrence—Leone must have noticed that the child was different from his young English cousins, who were also there on holiday at the time. What particularly disturbed him about Onorato was his apparent inability to show affection. "Our little boy really isn't 'demonstrative' and that often displeases me," was Vittoria's reply. "Perhaps it's our fault, we don't see him often enough. But he has many better qualities, after all! See him often, talk to him about me every now and again, and try to treat him in a more grown-up way … He has his own little ideas which only ask to be developed." And in another letter, written a few days later from Venice to an increasingly troubled Leone, Vittoria made a similar point: "He's very childish for his age, but I don't think that's a fault. I fear it's true that he is like me in many things, and that for this reason he'll never accomplish anything. But that means that at the end of his life he'll be able to say what I would like to have carved on my tombstone—I enjoyed myself."

As the days passed, however, Leone's letters became in-creasingly perturbed. Perhaps at the prompting of his relatives, he began to notice that Onorato walked badly, that he seemed lame, and that his spine was oddly curved. Vittoria was convinced that this was all an exaggeration: "What you tell me about the boy has troubled me a great deal, you're wrong to write such things when I'm far away and can't immediately see for myself if what you say is true. You speak as if he'd suddenly become a hunchback, a cripple and an imbecile!! Fortunately, such things do not show themselves all of a sudden like that and I console myself with the thought that I left him blooming not so long ago. It is true that he is a little backward for his age—but none of the doctors has ever told me that there was any reason to be worried about him."

Onorato Caetani, Vittoria and Leone's son, aged nineteen or twenty.

With the passing of time, though, the difficulties this only son of Vittoria Colonna and Leone Caetani (born exactly nine months after their wedding) experienced in both walking and learning became increasingly obvious. Operations in Switzerland, a made-to-measure orthopaedic mattress, daily gymnastic exercises—nothing seemed to work. As he grew up, Onorato's walk grew worse. He would not so much walk as run, but with his feet dragging and his back tilted to one side, and his large head lolling irreparably on his neck. In addition, a fault in the bone structure of his face made his nose run constantly and annoyingly, which in turn made him blush.

As an adolescent, Onorato would spend hours sitting at his desk, compiling lists of words taken from the dictionary or the encyclopaedia, without giving any sign that he really understood their meaning. He had a passion for the cinema, and at Vicobello—the sixteenth-century villa of his cousins, the Chigi-Zondadaris of Siena—we can still see the albums in which he collected press cuttings and stickers showing scenes from his favourite films, including many scenes in which the protagonists are kissing. From time to time the boy was overcome with rage and frustration: "Our characters are too similar," Vittoria wrote to Leone, "we both turn red and look at each other like angry roosters." But more often, Onorato demonstrated a mild, gentle nature: he loved music and dogs. He would burst out laughing over a mere trifle. And there were many things—Vittoria assured Leone in her letters—which he did understand.

"O's lessons are going much better," she wrote to her husband the day after she met Boccioni. "Basically he has a very good character, and even when I lose my temper and scold him formally, I later find him affectionate and smiling, without any resentment." And then she added, somewhat sadly, that if Leone could finally manage to spend a few days with them on the Isolino he would be able to see the improvement in their son for himself. "You will realise that he has qualities you perhaps did not suspect," she concluded.

Leone and Vittoria loved their only son dearly, but her letters hint at her fear that this sick boy was another reason why she was not accepted by the Caetanis. "Onorato and I seemed like two poor little flies leaving Palazzo Caetani," Vittoria wrote to Leone in 1911, relating the Duke her father in law's "coldness and indifference" on the day she left Rome to accompany her son to England, where he would be starting school for the first time. "I wondered if—apart from you—there would be anyone who would notice if we never came back. All this gave me a great desire to cry ... " Not for herself, she stressed, "but for the poor young thing who after all is the sole descendent of the Caetani house—of the last generation."

This was another reason for the subsequent bad blood between Vittoria and her sister-in-law Marguerite Chapin, the beautiful, cultured and rich American wife of Leone's youngest brother, the composer Roffredo. Marguerite, who after her marriage would assume the title of Princess of Bassiano, would give birth to two children: Lilia in 1913 and Camillo in 1915.

The first time the two sisters-in-law had an opportunity to get to know each other better was on a holiday at Engadine in the winter of 1911. Vittoria describes Marguerite as being excessively eager to appear shy and reserved—an unusual attitude "for an American woman of thirty, who has knocked about every hotel in Europe". In the rigidly class-bound society of the time, the Roman princess felt superior to her American sister-in-law. Soon, however, Marguerite, who "had, in those days, the sparkle and bloom of youth as well as the swift grace of movement and the beauty of finely drawn bones" (to quote the words of her friend, the writer Iris Origo, another American transplanted to Italy), would arouse strongly antagonistic feelings in Vittoria. Many letters to Leone reveal her displeasure at the fact that the Princess of Bassiano had managed to establish a good relationship with her in-laws. In addition, in the complex emotional balance of the Caetani clan, the children of Roffredo and Marguerite—handsome, healthy and intelligent—embodied the long-awaited future of the line. Lelia and Camillo quickly assumed the role of "favourite grandchildren", relegating "poor Onorato" for ever to the status of a sick relative.

Another factor that subsequently created rivalry between the sisters-in-law was Marguerite's intellectual energy. Like Vittoria, the Princess of Bassiano loved to surround herself with artists, writers and musicians. But whereas Vittoria, partly through a lack of real culture and partly through a rigidity due perhaps to her insecurity, would never succeed in coming down off her aristocratic pedestal, and would always remain on the margins of the twentieth century's intellectual and artistic currents, Marguerite would plunge into them wholeheartedly. In the 1920s in France (for many years the Prince and Princess Bassiano lived in Versailles) she founded, with the help of Paul Valéry and other intellectuals, the literary review *Commerce*. Among the contributors was Marguerite's cousin, the young T S Eliot. Finally, in Rome in the years after the Second World War (perhaps partly as a way of overcoming her grief at the death of her twenty-five-year-old son), Marguerite and the then very young Giorgio Bassani would found the review *Botteghe Oscure* (from the name of the street where Palazzo Caetani was situated), whose contributors included some of the greatest names in twentieth-century literature, such as Truman Capote, Tennessee Williams and Italo Calvino.

From the spring of 1903, just a year after the birth of her son, Vittoria, as we have seen, was often away on her travels. Sometimes she travelled alone and sometimes with friends: anything so not to have to spend months on end at Palazzo Caetani. She kept "the grey days of sadness and melancholy" at bay with a mixture of veronal and strong emotions. Her salvation lay in finding a glimmer of beauty in all things. From Salsomaggiore, where she went to treat her asthma, she wrote: "I am trying to take an interest in the smallest things—I stop in front of ugly little houses to admire the irises peeping out through the gate and go to find the flowers in the hedges without looking beyond them … " She would organise automobile excursions around Europe. An invitation to Buckingham Palace, or to spend a weekend at Windsor Castle, was more than enough reason to drop everything and leave at once for London.

In Rome, too, where she was lady-in-waiting to Queen Elena, Vittoria threw herself headlong into the social whirl. "In those days there were balls and receptions every evening," she would write, recalling those carefree years before the war. She was attracted to the world of writers and artists, and became friendly with Eleonora Duse and Gabriele d'Annunzio. Above all, she loved to have her portrait done by artists, such as the sculptor Carlo Fontana and the painter Boldini: "I loved the atmosphere of a studio," she would write with studied innocence, "I found the smell of turpentine and oil paints delightful!"

Almost every morning, Vittoria would escape to take painting lessons from a French artist named Noël, who had a studio in the Via Rasella. In the drawing rooms of Rome, it was whispered that, as well as being master and pupil, the two of them were also lovers. Noël, having enlisted in the French army, died in October 1914, leaving a wife and small children. Vittoria heard about it three weeks after taking possession of 'her' Isolino. It was the first event connected with the war to have a major impact on her. In a letter to her husband she confessed: "I am so afraid of falling back into my black melancholy without my work. This business has made me so sad that if it were not for you and O I would have no wish to return to Rome."

After the death of her teacher, Vittoria—who, as we have seen, had exhibited in a London gallery in 1909—stopped painting.

From now on, the garden on the Isolino would become her one creative project, and would remain so for many years. It was a kind of aesthetic refuge, a powerful antidote to dark thoughts.

"I went back again this morning," she wrote to her husband a few days after learning that the Isolino di San Giovanni was finally hers, "it is such a *bijou*, that little island—every day I discover a new corner ... There is nothing I would like to remove, to add perhaps yes, but nothing to change. I examined the house carefully, always thinking of you. I want you to have all your comforts. Do you want a study looking out on the lake or the greenery? I still can't believe my luck ... I'm sure you'll be happy on the island, you'll see! It's beautiful on all sides, and the country round about is a marvel. We'll have to have a little boat!"

The Borromeos, to judge from Vittoria's letters, were pleased that the Princess of Teano had come to their little island. One tangible sign of their approval was all the tables and marble fireplaces which they lent her to furnish the house. "The countess," she wrote enthusiastically, "will also give me turtle doves and white peacocks."

To Vittoria, the Isolino represented, at least initially, a possible way of saving a marriage already weakened by incompatibility and by family tensions. In the peace and quiet of her garden, she even imagined that she would be able to adapt to a simple, tranquil life in contact with nature, which would please Leone.

"It's important to live modestly," she wrote to him, knowing he would be pleasantly surprised. "No electric light—we will have long days there—a few oil lamps in the evening and a few candles—and that's enough. A bathroom? No. Each person will have a tub in his room, and I will see to it that there is plenty of hot water. The first expense will be to modernise the kitchen and the toilets. We must have white everywhere, and then—but you'll see it when it's done. We'll have a rustic little house which will be a delight."

In reality, her innate love of "comforts" as she called them, would always prevail over questions of style and economy. (Even when travelling by train across America in the 1930s, Vittoria would never forget to take her own sheets with her, embroidered with the family coat of arms and initials, as well as large bunches of fresh flowers to enliven the atmosphere of the carriage.)

What most drew Vittoria to the Isolino, though, was the thought that she would at last be able to create her own garden. In Fogliano, the vast Caetani estate on the Pontine Plain, there was a large garden, but that had been planted by her mother-in-law Ada, who had no intention of being helped by her daughter-in-law. "I did not like to go to Fogliano by myself," Vittoria would write years later in her memoirs, "as the duchess spent a good deal of time there industriously planting rows and rows of palm trees, and countless round flower beds in the garden which she made in front of the house, and I was made to feel that my visits were not welcome."* At Palazzo Caetani in Rome, there was no space for a garden. Vittoria had managed, admittedly, to get her hands on the palace's one terrace, which was small but sunlit, and she and Leone had amused themselves filling it with English roses and jasmines. But her passion for gardening could not be satisfied merely with a few plants in a vase.

"The idea of finally having a garden, and one that resembles the garden of my dreams," Vittoria wrote to Leone in a letter on the seventh of September 1914, "delights me. I feel that now I will have happy summers and autumns. And besides, with this war on, where could we go next year? There, we will have peace and quiet, then, when Europe has calmed down, we'll be really close to Switzerland, to Paris, even on the direct route to London. We couldn't find a more ideal summer home."

One of the first things that Vittoria did on the Isolino was to remove a palm tree that was close to the house. "You know how much I hate palms," she wrote to her husband, "and you can

* In English in the original.

imagine with what joy I cut it down." A joy made particularly delightful by the fact that the solitary palm on the island reminded her of those hundreds of American palms which her mother-in-law, with typically Victorian taste, had planted at Fogliano. She also moved two small granite columns which she and Leone had discovered behind a cypress hedge during one of his rare visits. She had them placed in front of the main door in such a way as to create an arbour: "It was a great effort," she wrote to Leone, "because of the rock, the bricklayer had to blow it up with a mine." The final effect, however, was to her liking. She found that it gave the house a "very artistic" touch. Vittoria also had the branches of the trees pruned because, she explained, they obscured the view of the lake.

Whenever, in the first years of her marriage, she had been overcome with anxiety in the "dark" Palazzo Caetani, Vittoria had spent her days bent over her photograph albums, drawing magnificent frames in watercolour to create a *trompe l'œil* effect, as if to embellish, or transform, a reality that had not lived up to expectations. Now once again, while "friends and acquaintances are dying every day" on various fronts, Vittoria took refuge from her grief in the only way she knew how: by concentrating on details, creating an elaborate frame for her life. "I don't want to think about it" is a phrase that often appears in her letters. During the war years, Vittoria would plant tirelessly. And many of these plants—citrus, camellias, rhododendrons and hydrangeas— came from the Borromeo nurseries on Isola Madre.

"You will understand from all this that I am in a very good mood, more than you think!" Vittoria had announced to Leone in October 1914. "Having a garden is like realising a dream. I would like to be living in my little house already and to be able to spend long hours with my flowers. You'll see how happy we will be there! You don't realise it, but afterwards it will seem to us that we have wasted these past thirteen summers."

Leone would, as it turned out, spend very little time on the Isolino. His first visit was in the autumn of 1914 to sign the rental contract with the Borromeos. He went back briefly the following year. During the summer of 1915, he wrote to her from Rome that he could not travel for the moment because he had very bad stomach pains. Vittoria replied curtly, "As for your not coming I won't say any more. Nella* tells me that you are fine, in good colour and eating well, so if you don't come it's because you don't want to." By this time, his relationship with the soubrette Ofelia Fabiani, twenty-eight years his junior, had already begun—a clandestine affair like many others, which might have remained so if the events of that summer of 1916 had not brought unmanageable feelings to the surface. Be that as it may, Leone and Vittoria, despite that constant flow of letters, had spent more time apart in the past few years than they had under the same roof.

That seventh of June, the Princess of Teano wrote to her husband that the "Futurist Boccioni" was coming for a visit to the Isolino, and that he would probably not like it. As it turned out, Boccioni was as enchanted by the tiny island as he was fascinated by its queen, Vittoria.

In the days that followed, the two met almost daily. The prevailing bad weather—storms and cold winds—prevented Boccioni from painting in the open air as much as he would have liked, so he had time to devote himself to Vittoria. She would often go to lunch at the Casanovas. He went to see her regularly. He would help her with bedding plants, and making sure the gates worked well. He tried to persuade her to create a 'Futurist' hen house painted in primary colours, and helped her to arrange the garden furniture.

"Yesterday Boccioni came to see me," Vittoria wrote to Leone on the twelfth of June. "He's delighted with the Isolino which I would have thought was too old- fashioned for his taste."

* Giovannella Caetani, Leone's sister.

Boccioni, she added, was really inspired by the little island. "He would like to paint us," she announced, flattered, "and I am encouraging him, wondering what on earth will come out! He's coming back tomorrow, weather permitting. At the moment, the thunder is making the whole house shake!"

Leone—to judge from his wife's letters—seemed ever more distant, an ethereal presence in her life. In the middle of June, he moved from his posting at Cortina d'Ampezzo to higher in the mountains, where the military observatory was situated.

"I was very interested in your description of the Austrian you were able to make out so clearly—do you think he could see you too?" Vittoria wrote to him. "I have thought of you especially on these days of such exceptionally bad weather—even here it was really cold, and while it was raining buckets, the mountains were covered in snow. When I was in my big soft bed, you must have been a lot less comfortable than me!"

The letters Vittoria wrote to Leone that June are strewn with fleeting but joyful allusions to Umberto Boccioni, their excursions together, and his visits to the Isolino. They are ambiguous letters, in which Vittoria, although omitting the most intimate details, seems to have wanted to share with her husband what was happening to her. Was she trying to make him jealous? Or begging him for forgiveness in advance? It is hard to understand her true intentions. But even in the past, whenever an important man had grown close to her—Edward VII, the Aga Khan, Winston Churchill—Vittoria had hastened to inform her husband by letter.

In any case, Vittoria's letters to Leone provide us with a precise chronology of her encounters with Boccioni. We discover for example that on Tuesday the thirteenth of June—exactly one week after they had met at Villa San Remigio—Vittoria Colonna and Umberto Boccioni spent their first evening alone together on the Isolino. This was not an easy thing to arrange, because, as we learn from a letter by Boccioni, the Casanovas expected the artist to dine with them and the Busonis every evening at Villa San Remigio.

There would be a full moon on the night of the thirteenth of June, and Vittoria had suggested to Umberto that he should come and see it from her island. Before that, they would enjoy the sunset together and then eat in the open air on the terrace overlooking the lake. At the time, the garden was "full of the scents of lilies, jasmine and verbena." From the Isolino, in the evening, the lights could be seen shining on the opposite shore of the lake and, closer, those of the grand hotels of Stresa, against the dark background of the mountain that towered over them.

As usual, Vittoria had prepared everything down to the last detail: the simple but excellent food—vegetables from the kitchen garden and small fish from the lake—the candles ready to be lit, the wine. The house was full of flowers. That summer, in addition to the vases of white roses and hydrangeas, Vittoria had got into the habit of placing bunches of sweet peas around the rooms in small glass or silver tumblers. She was proud of these colourful flowers, which came from her garden—she had had the seeds sent from England the previous autumn and had planted them everywhere, and now they were blooming ("It was almost with emotion that I picked my first!" she had written to Leone). In summer the windows were wide open and the light wind from the lake spread the scent of the flowers into every room.

"He made himself pleasant and interesting," she wrote to her husband two days later about her first evening spent with Boccioni on the Isolino, "without any pose, but it was cold, so the moonlight was *raté*, and we spent the evening in the drawing room with the lights on. He is delighted with the Isolino, as is everyone who comes here. The little house is so fresh, so scented with the flowers that I had put everywhere in abundance, and although everything is Italian, it feels for some reason like an English cottage."

Vittoria's letters to her husband became a little less frequent in this period. Instead of once a day, she wrote to him once every two or three days. She also changed the way she signed, from "your loving Vittoria" to the more lukewarm "your Vittoria".

On the eighteenth of June she wrote to him: "My darling, you will receive this at about the time of our wedding anniversary, and I imagine that that day you will think of me perhaps a little more than usual. And I will do the same on my side. As fate would have it, in fifteen years we've spent few of these anniversaries together, I don't think more than four or five at most … "

Then, after the usual meteorological details—"the climate here is behaving in an exceptional way, no one can remember a June like this"—Vittoria told her husband about Boccioni's latest evening visit (this time not spoilt by the bad weather): "Two days ago it was ideal, I don't remember if I wrote to you about it—Boccioni came for dinner and I took him back in a boat in the moonlight; the Isolino was truly fantastic that evening with its dark cypresses and the scent of magnolia and jasmine … "

The good weather seems to have gained the upper hand at last. The roses were in full bloom, as were the snapdragons on the borders of the English meadow. During his stay at San Remigio, Boccioni made several further trips to the Isolino for dinner. On the evening of the twenty-second of June, Vittoria invited him to meet her mother. There was also another guest, a man named Massara, perhaps a friend of the artist's. Teresa Caracciolo and Umberto Boccioni got on well, and after dinner they all remained outside on the terrace, chatting and smoking cigarettes, until late at night. Subsequently, Umberto would frequently send regards to Vittoria's mother in his letters.

Was Vittoria Colonna falling in love with the soldier-painter? It is hard to say. Of the hundreds of letters she wrote to her husband in the course of twenty years or more of marriage, however, it is undeniable that those written from the Isolino in the summer of 1916, before Umberto Boccioni's death, are imbued with a joy and freshness that are practically unique.

"Today is a wonderful day," she writes for example in mid-June, "and I really hope that it is the same where you are. The lake is blue and sparkling, and from the bottom of the garden, against a cloudless sky, I can see the mountains of the Simplon, with their tops all white with snow. The morning walk, with my basket on my arm! It was much enjoyed, in fact today I found a lot of things to do and worked from nine until lunch, and I shan't hide the fact that afterwards, I had a little nap, lying on the terrace with many soft cushions!!"

Since Boccioni had entered her life, Vittoria's restlessness had given way to a deep sense of being rooted. "I feel that my true home is now here," she wrote to Leone, "in this little white house and this green island!!"

Over the course of the month of June, Umberto Boccioni worked energetically at his portrait of Busoni. He was trying to make things ever more concise and pared-down, he wrote to his friend and supporter Vico Baer, a member of a rich, cultivated Jewish family in Milan. Meeting Vittoria and getting to know her had aroused in him waves of emotion which stirred his creativity. This was not the first time that the presence and proximity of a woman had generated in him an intense desire to work. Years earlier, he had written about Ines: " ... Her body arouses in me continual harmonies, so that with every movement I feel the urge to draw ... " Something similar happened with Vittoria and the portrait of Busoni. As the work progressed and Boccioni's visits to the Isolino increased, the colours in the painting became more compact and vivid,

Umberto Boccioni, Portrait of Ferruccio Busoni (1916). Galleria d'Arte Moderna, Rome.

with a predominance of green, ultramarine and electric blue. The brushstrokes were full and dynamic. The painter attacked the canvas with overflowing energy, almost aggressively, transforming burgeoning emotions into vibrant colours and powerful brushstrokes. The portrait of Busoni is a portrait imbued with happiness.

"First he would play, with fingers that were not fingers," Boccioni would write to a friend about the experience. "And then I would paint with brushes that were no longer brushes, and with fingers that moved of their own accord … I don't know how the portrait came out, among other things, as a good likeness, painted as it was in a state of mind that was completely outside reality."

Boccioni must have entered Vittoria's solitude with the same impetuosity that pervades his last great painting: full of ideas, full of desires. He and Vittoria had decided that, as soon as the portrait was finished, he would move to her house for a few days to work. The Isolino was an ideal meeting place and he had entered her rarefied harmony with a mixture of enthusiasm and surprising tenderness.

Everything on Vittoria's island interested him: the flowers, the kitchen garden. Even the look of the hen house, as we have mentioned, became the object of animated aesthetic discussions: "He made it really well," Vittoria wrote to Leone, describing the hen house as recently completed by Italo, "and he painted it green, which horrified the Futurist Boccioni, who says that the colour is too dull. He wanted me to make the roof red and the posts blue but I refused."

In the letters which Boccioni would write to Vittoria in the following weeks, we also find numerous allusions to the person he called "[his] young friend". Onorato Caetani had turned fourteen that April, and his mother noted that he was becoming such a "strange little character" that it was difficult to know what he liked and what he didn't. During his repeated visits to the Isolino, Boccioni showed a great interest in Onorato. He liked that capricious boy who had difficulty in expressing himself and in moving, but who was also gentle, affectionate, and as curious as a young child.

Onorato spent much of his time on the Isolino, Vittoria told her husband, compiling his usual lists: "endless lists of painters, musicians, mountains, rivers, or battles, etc. Always alphabetical lists with many dates done now with quite a lot of care." He had just had yet another operation to help him breathe better through his nose, allowing him to close his mouth. The boy became very attached to Umberto Boccioni. Accustomed to living isolated from his contemporaries, his only companions—apart from his somewhat distracted mother— being the tutors and servants paid to look after him, he must have considered the interest shown in him by Boccioni, so dear to his mother, a cause for pride. As Vittoria wrote to Leone with a certain amusement, Onorato had really conceived "a great passion" for the painter "and followed him everywhere like a puppy".

Boccioni, for his part, found Onorato "an original character", as he told Vittoria. One day, he even made her cry (a fact she duly mentioned to her husband) by reproaching her for her mistakes in bringing up Onorato, an exceptional boy whom she tormented, in his opinion, with her excessive strictness. Whenever he stopped compiling his lists, the boy would run from one side of the island to the other, shouting at the top of his voice "Goethe! Goethe!" Strolling alone with Boccioni, one metre ninety tall, he would open up like a flower, in a way he had probably never done with anyone. "A good friend always ready to help," Vittoria would write to Boccioni during that summer. "It is a characteristic of yours which I like, just like your kindness to my son, for whom your friendship could do a lot later on." Indeed, when he was with Boccioni, Vittoria wrote to Leone,

Onorato was becoming better at communicating—not only with gestures, but also with words. Umberto encouraged him to express himself, telling Vittoria that the boy was not stupid, that the questions he asked were sensible ones. Onorato's vitality, his plucky cheerfulness, sensitivity and solitude seem to have touched deep chords in Umberto Boccioni.

"He sees him as the Futurist boy!" Vittoria wrote, incredulously, to Leone. "Naturally he disapproves of the way he lives. But what can I do? It's easy to say that he should have intelligent friends who develop his ideas with conversation—but where do I find them?"

At the end of June, once Busoni's portrait was finished, Boccioni returned to Milan. At the time, the pages of the newspapers were full of the "Italian advance", which seemed, after weeks of bloody combat, to be making progress along the front between the Adige and the Brenta. In a letter to his "dear, tremendous friend" Busoni, written in Milan on the twenty-ninth of June, Boccioni says that he is "still feeling the effects of my stay", which had reawakened in him "infinite contacts, dulled lately for many reasons which it is pointless to enumerate." "It reconciled me to the country and to solitude," he confessed to his friend. From an artistic point of view, it had been a productive period: "In a few days I had gone through various stages and was well on my way to finding the right style. I needed to stay." He immediately added: "I hope to go back to the Isolino, just for a few days."

"I hope to go back to the Isolino … " he had written, vaguely. But in fact everything was already arranged: Boccioni would remain in Milan for only two days, just enough time to put his studio in order, see his mother, and pack his bags.

On the morning of the first of July 1916 (the same day, and at more or less the same time as the start of the battle of the Somme, in which more than a million men would die) Boccioni left his house-studio in Porta Romana to see Vittoria again. He took the eight o'clock train, which arrived at Pallanza-Fondo Toce at ten eighteen. In the newspapers, that morning, he read that, despite the torrential rain beating down on the eastern front, the Russian army was continuing its advance, bringing hope to the Allies.

On his arrival, Boccioni found Vittoria waiting for him outside the station in her automobile. With her was Emilio, her and Leone's driver. Apart from his suitcase with his clothes and a few books, Boccioni had with him paper, paints and perhaps one or two small canvases. The object of that visit, they had told each other many times, was to prolong the atmosphere of peace and serenity which, during those last weeks at San Remigio, had made it possible for him to paint with renewed vigour.

Vittoria, too, had woken early. The day was radiant and she felt happy, despite the fact that the atmosphere in the house was somewhat grim. The previous day news had come that good old Italo, Gertie's husband as well as an invaluable helper on the Isolino—"He did everything," Vittoria wrote to Leone, "tutor, cook, carpenter!"—would also have to leave very soon for the front. That morning, however, Vittoria was unable to contain her joy. "After all," she wrote to Leone, "there is a war on, and it could be worse. Provided it finishes soon and you all come back home! It seems to me there is nothing else to wish for in the world. I devour the newspapers, and I hope, I hope so much! It seems to me there's a general optimism in the air. If I were a believer, how I would pray in these times! It must be such a great consolation. Instead I go to my garden, among my flowers, and try to forget the anguish of waiting."

In this same letter, Vittoria informed her husband that the "Futurist Boccioni" would be spending a few days with her. She could hardly fail to do so. There were too many people, starting with her chauffeur Emilio, who might have reported back to Leone or another of the Caetanis—it would surely have looked very suspicious if she had omitted to mention it.

Vittoria, however, made only a brief reference to the matter, and indeed, she told Leone, perhaps lying, that the artist's visit would be a brief one: "Today Boccioni is coming for two days: his plan to stay longer, and do a lot of painting, went up in smoke because he was born in the third four-month period of '82, which means they've called him too."

A few hours later, having consoled Gertie for Italo's imminent departure and given orders that everything should be made ready for Boccioni's arrival, Vittoria went to the station to pick up her friend.

The day was hot—"the sun is burning"—and despite the war the beaches between Pallanza and Stresa were swarming with bathers.

Umberto and Vittoria reached the Isolino a couple of hours before lunch. They had just enough time to change and go down to the beach for a bathe. The chambermaid Emilia was laying the table on the veranda, and the garden, thanks to the dense vegetation, was cool and shady in contrast to the white heat of the day.

Vittoria had had one of the most beautiful rooms in the house made ready for the artist: the green one, which looked out on the terrace of English roses and jasmine and on one of the most spectacular views of the lake. The room had also been filled with fresh flowers from the garden. On the little wooden table, a tray of fruit had been placed, with a little plate, silver cutlery and a tablecloth with an entwined *V* and *C*.

From that moment, for an entire week, Umberto Boccioni and Vittoria Colonna would enjoy the solitude of the Isolino, far from prying eyes—or at least so they thought. The days passed slowly and idly in the summer heat. Umberto would sleep late in the morning. At lunch, invigorated by the cool water of the lake, they would eat beneath the pergola and then from there observe the succession of hot hours and the passing ferries. In the evening, after sunset, they would often dine alone by candlelight and then would lie down on the sofa on the veranda where they would spend their time looking up at the sky and smoking. It was here perhaps that their love began, among those great soft cushions which—in their secret language—they dubbed "Futurist cushions".

They talked a lot. "You talked to me about so many interesting things and explained some that I had never understood before," she would write to him after that first stay on the island.

The opportunities for love multiplied. It was inevitable: Umberto Boccioni was a sensual man, an enthusiast for what he called "the complete, impulsive life", believing in its absolute superiority over platonic love. In his youthful diaries, where he even noted down the names of those who gave him "exceptional pleasure", we find many references to his erotic adventures. And Boccioni's presence seems to have reawakened in Vittoria what Leone called her "pagan" temperament, devoted to pure pleasure. "When one lives without faith, without fear and without hope," she herself had written to her husband a few years earlier, "one must enjoy life as much as possible."

It is likely, though, at least at the beginning, that Vittoria greeted Boccioni's advances with a certain hesitancy. In a letter written about a month later, the artist would retrace the "wonderful crescendo" of their love which had finally flowed into a "chaste pleasure", and would speak unambiguously of their "infinite communion of body and spirit".

What there is between us is a profound reality, it was born as a reality. However recently we had met, and become friends … there is our secret, that wonderful crescendo which led us from chastity to chastity to our chaste pleasure! O, our nights! Your pallor, *your confusion, my terror, our infinite communion of body and spirit. My divine one, I feel that you love*

Vittoria with Max on the terrace of the Isolino (spring-summer 1916).

> *me, a little, a little more than when you measured me with avarice with*
> *the tip of your little finger … Do you remember?*

The physical love between Vittoria Colonna and Umberto Boccioni must, in fact, have begun quite rapidly, despite her initial "avarice". Her reticence was understandable, given the many difficulties standing in the way of their relationship: her marriage, her husband's public position, the many prying eyes that were certainly observing them on the island as well as on terra firma, Boccioni's imminent departure for the front, her fear of losing him—and perhaps also Vittoria's genuine surprise at such exuberance.

On the third of July Vittoria sent Leone a letter which reveals that Boccioni's original two days on the Isolino had become somewhat longer: "Since the day before yesterday I have had Boccioni here, and he's very upset at having to present himself on the tenth," she writes as if to divert attention from the Isolino to the war. "It isn't that he lacks courage, but he is absorbed in his art and this will cut short all his work. I believe that he is sincere in his theories, which I cannot yet accept, although he explained many things that had previously been incomprehensible to me. In a word, Futurism is beginning to interest me, and who knows, after the war, I may come down on their side! But this damned war has to end first!"

Umberto Boccioni's powers of persuasion, so extolled by Apollinaire and his Futurist friends, had again scored a hit: the Princess of Teano, or so it seems, was also caught up in the excitement of Futurism. During that last summer of his life, despite the crisis he had been going through and the figurative nature of his latest paintings, Boccioni—or so Vittoria wrote—had no intention of renouncing Futurism. On the contrary, to judge from the final paintings produced at Pallanza and the letters in which he describes them, Boccioni was intent on opening the door to new horizons, pushing the dynamic impulse of Futurism beyond the borders of mere style to reach its essence.

Umberto Boccioni remained on the Isolino as Vittoria's guest from the first to the eighth of July. The sunny day which had greeted him on his arrival was followed by others on which the weather was unsettled, as it had been in June. "It still can't be said," Vittoria wrote to Leone, "that the summer has really come—we pay for every two days of good weather with one of rain." At the end of that week, a cyclone hit the lake, bringing the same disorder and disturbance to Vittoria's garden that love had brought into her life.

Boccioni's plans for work during that week of uninterrupted privacy on the Isolino soon gave way to an all-pervading languor. "He hasn't had the courage to paint in the last few days," Vittoria wrote casually to her husband "and has spent his time sleeping!"

On the eighth of July, the date of his departure, Umberto and Vittoria went to lunch with the "always kind" (his words) Casanovas. In a letter written from Milan, the artist would tell his friend Busoni that they had all missed him that day at Villa San Remigio, and had been nostalgic for his passionate opinions on culture. "We were all a little terrified of you," he added with friendly irony.

That last day on the lake was, however, affected by a number of mishaps which nearly made Boccioni miss his train for Milan.

" … It was going so well and we had two or three lovely excursions," Vittoria wrote to her husband in dismay, "then yesterday I went with Boccioni to have lunch at the Casanovas— the automobile stopped as we were climbing the hill—never mind, we went up on foot. Afterwards, it was supposed to come and pick Boc up and take him to the station—it again stopped on the way up and there was no way of getting the engine started. When it finally made up its mind to leave, there was no question of being able to catch the train—we had to go back to the Isolino for another three hours! Then a second departure, and half-way the car stops again, without the excuse of the slope. It was awful. With great luck a tram passed and Boc—and his bags—arrived on time at the station, otherwise he would have missed the last train of the day! I came back on the tram … "

The next day, Sunday the ninth of July, Boccioni wrote Vittoria a letter overflowing with emotion and nostalgia:

Dear, kind friend

I arrived in Milan in a dreamy state! The summer evening, the fact that it was Saturday or my abrupt reawakening to reality gave Milan a restless, noisy, crowded air. I passed through the middle of the city's commotion as if distracted. The waters and the sky and the Isolino had left in me a blue-green harmony like the colours of your house. I felt a certain pride within me as if my life had acquired a greater depth. I felt pure and calm. Reconciled with the outside world, with myself, with everything. I felt grateful and more elevated. I felt that the meaning of my life and my aspirations had increased, as if your kindness had imposed a superior order on the turmoil of my sensibility. This state of mind is still with me and will always stay with me. The contact with your exquisite kindness and with your supreme gentleness must surely mark a decisive date in my life. I have said it! I will never tire of saying it! You have done me a great deal of good, no one has encouraged me to become *in the way you have! My affection and my respect and my gratitude live in the depths of my admiration. Every one of my gestures is affected by and will always be affected by your presence. I have come back a child, I am living in ecstasy, I have an almost religious sense of the inevitability of your friendship.*

When the train rounded a bend and took you away from my wave I ran to the end of the last carriage and saw you still crossing the track.

I had to hide the tears of my regret and my infinite tenderness from two fat bourgeois who were looking at me in astonishment. I reached Stresa. Isola dei Pescatori! Isola Madre! The Isolino!! I closed myself up in the sweetness of your last wave and called to you, I gave you all my fervent gratitude, I wished you all the joys and beauties and dominions of life. If the sincerity and fervour of distant affections depend on us you will have in me a continual safeguard. There is nothing left but art and your friendship. You have wiped out everything else. You are superior to me. Since yesterday I have not made a gesture without my mind immediately saying: Yes, this is worthy of her! Do not fear, my good dear friend, do not fear my letters. Everything you do and will do is pure and nothing is purer than my respect for you. What I feel is so great and elemental that any everyday word will express it. In other letters I will tell you about myself and my life. Today I want to tell you again how dear and how beautiful our friendship can become. No one has the right to refuse such a great pure thing. Last night I didn't go out. I talked a lot to my mother about you and I moved her and she thanks you for me!

Tomorrow morning I am going to answer the call. But I am calm and ready for any sacrifice. I have had a great deal in meeting you, it is right that I pay my debt of sacrifice to life. To leave my mother, and the studio, to interrupt the course of my life … Never mind! For you and for Italy, what will be, will be. If destiny wants my name to remain in something more than what I have done so far everything will come back. It doesn't matter, I am calm and ready. I have seen my studio, it already has the abandoned air of things that do not belong to us. It is sad but my mind has had such a bath of poetry that my joy is vibrant and alive in serenity.

Not an hour goes by without my saying: now she's in the garden, now she's embroidering, now she's having tea, now she's sending Onorato to study, now she's going up to her room! And all the episodes of the day, the smallest, the most insignificant, appear to me in a degree of harmony and beauty. I live as if in a daze and then whisper inside myself dear one! blessed one! blessed one!

My great and dear friend, how much I owe you! It pains me not to be able to link your image to projects for work, but everything will come in its time won't it? The war will not shatter anything, with us it will not have its inexorable force, I don't want it! It's terrible! I feel a little afraid!

Forgive me! My next letter will be calmer, but despite everything I'm writing to you I don't understand how one can escape the grip of despair. It is shameful for a man, with the war looming over us, with the sacrifices everyone is making, to grieve over an absence ... Do not think badly of me I am ready for everything but I am afraid in the dullness of the barracks of feeling all the horror and injustice of this separation. I have worked too much, I have dreamt too much of an ideal life of work and affection and beauty ... everything collapsing would give me the right to grieve: wouldn't it?

Forgive me. I have thrown down in one go everything I am writing. Don't judge me badly. Next time I'll be stronger, calmer, more cheerful. Be indulgent as always, smile and have no fear. Thank you, my sweet friend, my very harmonious friend, my radiant, beautiful hope. I feel the scent of the bay trees and the lemon grass!

I kiss your dear, good hands respectfully.

Your Boccioni.

What was Princess Colonna's reaction to such a torrential outpouring of words and feelings?

Was she flattered, disturbed, moved? Perhaps all those things, and perhaps also scared—as if (having lived for years torn between superficial flirtations that were more social than amorous and the calm detachment of her solitude) she felt unprepared for so much love. And may she not also have felt the impulse to retreat in the face of such ardour, to put the distance of good manners between herself and her impetuous lover?

We do not know, and all we can do is speculate. The fact remains that when she replied to Boccioni's letter on the tenth of July, the tone of her letter was very different from his.

Dear friend,

Thank you for such a beautiful and spontaneous letter which I've read and reread many times: not like the others I receive, which often remain unopened for days on end! It was strange to find myself alone again on the Isolino: after a week I had become accustomed to your company. You talked to me about so many interesting things and explained some that I had never understood before, I don't think we ever had a moment of boredom when we were together, did we? and now I miss you. *I who believed I had become so accustomed to solitude!*

I understand how strange it must have seemed to you to be back in Milan after that interlude in your life ... 'interlude' isn't the right word and I already seem to see you knitting your brows! It will probably be the beginning of a long friendship in which we may be able to do a lot *together, for ourselves and for our Italy. You will need to educate me; I'll be a docile pupil, you'll see ... But for now these are dreams, the reality is the war and the fact that you have to leave as a soldier, breaking off everything, art, friendship, for God knows how many months, and what will happen before we see each other again! You have the presentiment that we will meet again very soon—I don't know—but I hope so. In fact I see nothing clearly, not even my own existence these last few days. I know nothing—I let myself be dragged along by fate. I go back to my flowers, my strolls along the avenues, with my basket on my arm, followed by Max. I even try* not *to think, but that's not so easy. As you see, I am in a somewhat confused state of mind!—that's why my letter is not clear, because I am trying to be oh so sincere! The only thing that seems to me perfectly definite and clear is that I believe in you, in your honesty and sincerity and talent: that* I respect you. *I am very ambitious for you, now that we are friends, terribly ambitious. You have to climb, climb! Make yourself recognised by everyone. And in the meantime be a soldier. But even that is beautiful, and I would not want you not to do it: and anyway it would not be possible to shirk your duty, it is not in your character, although no one would have more right than you to want it, you who live for art.*

I hope that you will soon tell me the results of your medical examination, and if you defer it for a month it will be granted. In any case, continue to make those notes, like the ones you read to me, and which I liked very much, now that painting is out of the question, work on that other branch of art which is very useful. If ever you return here, and we can be undisturbed, we will work in the little cell which is close to the drawing room: I will sit down at the desk and you in the armchair: you will dictate, and in this way we will spend hours that must no longer be idle and great things will be done, you will see! You will see! It seems to me that you must write a lot more, because that is very useful: it helps your ideas and theories to be more deeply understood: your books ought to be translated: have you ever thought of an English translation? The English public is slow but serious. As you know better than I, if it grasps an idea it grasps it seriously, and it would be an excellent preparation for a future exhibition in London, for example.

You see that I am full of latent energies. You laugh at my state of catalepsy (is that how it's written?) but you don't know that I am also capable of feverish activity if I am enthusiastic about something.

Dear friend—these are plans for a remote and hazy future. Now tell me how your life will be, how it is, and give me lots of details. I'm interested in everything.

I reach out both hands to you, in friendship and affection

Vittoria Colonna

On the morning of Monday the tenth of July, Umberto presented himself at the barracks for his medical examination. We can only speculate whether or not he was secretly hoping that he would be sent home again. But it was not to be—his slight pulmonary emphysema, aggravated by excessive smoking and by a recent bronchial illness, did not exempt him from being enlisted in the field artillery. (In fact, as he would write to Vittoria, not without a touch of coquetry, "[his] ... statuesque body made a great impression".) His destination was as yet unknown, but in the meantime his levy was given leave until the twenty-fourth of July. "So I have twelve whole days before me," he wrote to Vittoria, unable to conceal his joy.

At the time, the newspapers were printing encouraging headlines about the Russian, English and French offensives. The Allied advance, it was said, was "proceeding victoriously". By the end of that summer, the battle of the Somme alone had left more than a million dead—Tommies, *poilus*, *turcos* (the name given to the colonial soldiers involved in the conflict), and *boches*—plus two million wounded. Meanwhile, in the amphitheatre of mountains between the Adige and the Brenta, the Italian forces (Leone among them) continued their tug of war with the Austrians. But not a word of this appears in the letters between Boccioni and Vittoria.

During these days, Umberto wrote to Vittoria on the twelfth of July, *I will finish off everything that cannot be left interrupted and then I will be free. I am even distracted while I write. It seems impossible to me!! I will have at least one week free. What shall I do? I await your advice. Perhaps a week is exaggerated? Perhaps four days ... The Casanovas kindly invited me, in case I had leave, but I said it would be very difficult. It would hurt me to be so close to the Isolino and yet so far.*

You know what my dream would be! But since you have guessed it, I do not have the courage to formulate it. I understand the need to avoid malign interpretations, of which there may not be any (you are too elevated!) but my departure which cannot be postponed, the necessity of seeing Colonel Talamo, now my direct superior, the very strong wish to go back and thank you and greet you with the exquisite princess Colonna and the Casanovas could encourage me to return for two days which could then become four and five. Who knows when such a possibility would be repeated, don't you think?

I have been taken to task for not having visited Isola Bella. To go down every day from San Remigio and return for dinner, etc., spoils everything. Think about it, dear friend, I await your orders, which will be carried out completely, as always.

Your letter, I confess, was awaited with indescribable anxiety! As always, you went further than I expected, and the words you have for my art and my future have made me throb with pride and gratitude!

I am very moved by that and it seems to me that I'm beginning to obtain with your friendship that reward and the beginning of that recognition which my efforts and my love of art have ardently dreamt of! Thank you, thank you, my great, good friend! What I have to do has only just begun! Everything is still to come and everything will be great and pure. Much of it will be your work. I met you at a moment of crisis in my methods, in my friends, in everything! You have illuminated me, you have given me back a purpose, you have created order, you have inflamed my hope, ennobled my ambition!

If I return to tell you these things on the Isolino, who can think badly of it? I see the little harbour with the green vases and the blue flowers. I see the lights of Stresa, Mount Mottorone, and the sleepy sister islands. I see green and blue! They are the colours of my painting. The green of my hope, the blue of my dreams! Since I returned, I have been a new man. The mysterious influence of a harmonious friendship! Who could think badly of that?

Will you let me come? I am living distractedly, waiting, write to me immediately I beg you. The purity of my feelings surrounds you like the blue glory of the lake lapping against the shores of the sweet, dear little island.

Everything is blue and large, clear and very green. Milan weighs on me. What, today, do I have in common with the anxieties of city life? I'll be better off among the horses and the cannons. Everything is blue and large, clear and very green!

I haven't made any more notes. The thread of my ideas has been interrupted. It will resume. I have had to, and still have to, run here, there and everywhere. I have to write letters and leave everything in order. Even though I'm not working—which is not my fault—I'm still worthy of you! I think of you all the time and try to make my life and the acts that go with it worthy of the nobility of the feelings you have inspired in me.

...

Farewell, incomparable friend. Thank you for your kind words and always keep your respect for me. Write to me I beg you about what I must do!

I kiss your hands respectfully!

Your very devoted Boccioni.

On the back of one of the sheets, written across the whole page, Boccioni adds: "Thoughtlessly, I left these pages blank. I fill them ideally with all that a devoted soul full of admiration for you can say. I received the boxes of paints. In one of them there was a *Daily Mail* which you were reading on the Isolino. This was enough to move me and made me think of days gone by. I am keeping it! Your Boccioni."

That same evening, having received a box full of fresh flowers gathered for him by Vittoria on the Isolino, Boccioni wrote to her again.

My friend!

I can't resist writing a few lines. The box of flowers arrived. All the poetry of the Isolino, of its bushes, all the poetry of your kindness was contained in those four strips of wood. Having opened the box I saw it all again and I was overwhelmed by an inconsolable nostalgia.

My mother was deeply moved and immediately wanted to send you a telegram. How good you are, my dear friend.

I have had a sad day. Milan seems to me empty and dark. I feel distant from everything and everybody. I've re-read your letter, I've meditated on my plans, I've kept it with me tonight, I've re-read it and I've thanked you again from the depths of my adoration.

If I can't go back and see you, then I'd rather leave today for the regiment. There's no point in staying here any longer! There is something that's taking hold of me! grabbing me by the throat and moving me! I wander the streets disgusted with everything. Everything seems to me banal and poor and pointless and vulgar. I will calm down my friend, I will calm down have no fear. Nothing will be done that

*Image from a postcard sent by Vittoria to Boccioni (July 1916). On the back:
"Greetings from the Isolino. Come back and see us soon! Vittoria."*

*could offend your honesty, your peace, your respect for me, the supreme
beauty of your life!*

*But I feel that something is overflowing in me! What a grey day in
this heavy heat! Soon evening will fall on the dear island. Will you be
on the veranda? Or in the white and blue drawing room? Certainly you
will climb the secret staircase silently and majestically. You will enter your
room … Goodnight, my friend, smile in your sleep.*

I kneel and kiss your hands

Your Boccioni.

No sooner had Vittoria received the letter in which he announced that he would be free until the twenty-fourth than she
seemed all at once to throw caution to the winds—it was almost
as if that unexpected passion at a time of war had made the
Princess of Teano lose her deeply rooted sense of form and
convention. Her desire to see Boccioni again comes through
strongly in the letter she wrote to him that same twelfth of July.

Dear friend,

*I have just come back from Intra and found your letter waiting for me. I
read it all straight through, sitting on the veranda, because I knew that
you would have so many things to tell me that would interest me. So you
are to be an artilleryman, and you are free until the 24th … and you are
pleased. I say immediately: come as soon as you can. We may not be able
to see each other again for such a long time, and in this year of war I hope
that people will have other things to think about than to observe that you
like being on the Isolino. I will say that, having to talk to Colonel Talamo
(good heavens, you will find something to tell him!) you asked me if you can
come back for three days. These three can then be prolonged. Anyway it's
no one else's business how long you stay with me! Later I will have other
friends, who will stay even longer. So wire me the day and the hour of your
arrival, and if you are coming by boat or train. I am waiting for you!*

*It may be that Carlo Visconti will come, he told me he was coming on
11th July but hasn't been in touch again. But you will find him cultured*

and friendly. He is not in good health and often has to go to bed before lunch and even stay in his room all day, the poor man. He's an old friend and I like him a lot; an honest soul.

So I will see you again, having resigned myself to resuming my solitary life. There is a moon, you will see what a marvel it is if you come back soon! We will have wonderful evenings. Last night, when I went to bed, there was a fantastic streak of silver on the lake: like the paillettes *that we used to wear. I started to read your book! There are a number of things I need to ask you about, then when sleep came I looked at your portrait on the first page and said, "Goodnight my friend"—and fell asleep.*

I have seen no one since you left apart from my mother. No, I'm wrong; a couple of neighbours, from Belgirate, rather; who called the Isolino "Very chic!" That says it all.

The prefect gave me a few first photographs, but they are badly printed. I will send you one though.

Until we meet again, my friend. Very soon, I think?

Both hands
Vittoria Caetani di Teano.

His reply, written on the thirteenth or fourteenth of July, is a hymn of gratitude and joy.

My good friend!
Just received photographs and letter! Thank you! thank you! thank you! I am throbbing all over with affection and admiration! My beautiful and sweet and dear one! I saw the Isolino … I will see it again, perhaps on Sunday, perhaps Saturday it's beautiful it's tremendous! I can't bear to think about it! Two extraordinary things have happened since I left! My presentiment that I would see you again soon has come true. I too wrote yesterday evening and whispered with infinite tenderness: goodnight my friend! You wrote the same thing to me. There is something so harmonically linked in our acts, I'm quite staggered! And I make mad proposals for the future and they won't be mad! They will be beautiful realities, my friend! my purity! my beauty! sweetness, perfume, ecstasy! With you everything

is possible! It pains me not to be able to tell you by letter all the beautiful things I feel. I fear I am not worthy I'm not up to the task either now while I write or tomorrow on the Isolino. But you will encourage me you will have one of your silent gestures which electrify me. Which give me courage! If not you know with you I become shy and childlike. And because you inflame what is deepest and purest in me, what is noblest in me as a man and as an artist! You alone could read in my thoughts and not a single feeling would you find that is not addressed to you! That does not look to you as to a light! If you read in my soul you would be proud of the dream you have created in me! Goodnight my friend! I am writing in haste so that I can post this tomorrow.

Your Boccioni.

In the days immediately preceding his return to the Isolino, Boccioni sent Vittoria two more letters. The first must have been written on the evening of the fourteenth of July:

Dear Princess,

It is eight in the evening and I am going to bed. I'm not well, I feel feverish. But it's nothing. I'm leaving on Sunday morning. I would have liked to hear from you if you prefer me to arrive by boat or from Fondotoce. It goes without saying that you won't be put out in any way. If I don't hear from you telling me what you'd like, I will wire you where I am arriving, and when.

Last night, the moon was magnificent! These evenings and these nights are almost unbearable to me. I feel alone even when I am with my friends. I seem to be following centuries-old habits. People and things seem to me worthless, grey, evanescent, pointless. Words empty and foolish … I live, chatter and think of other things … I think of an emerald in a lake of cobalt. I whisper to myself tender words like the green of the traditional poets, but that's how it is. I live in ultramarine! I say good, small things that someone must hear. Has Signor Visconti arrived? Today I was hoping to receive a letter from you. Not seeing anything I assumed your guest had arrived and you were even busier than before.

…

I have a terrible headache, my friend. I must break off. In my mind the source of feeling never dries up. It rises, it keeps rising and submerges me. Every evening at this hour I have an attack of languor that surprises even me. People talk to me and I whisper to myself words of infinite tenderness. My eyes burn, I close them, and I let myself go, down, down, in an infinite flight plané. *Am I boring you? Am I repeating myself? That may be inevitable given the* immutability *of my affection!*

As soon as I'm a soldier I'll write other things. For now let me say … You have listened to me so much with that long serene slightly stern face, which fills me with such awe … Forgive me and smile!

Farewell my great and dear friend. Regards to Onorato and silence him with your sweetness … and in Italian.

I hear him cry: Goethe! (Is that how it's written?) I see Max making you nervous with his flower-killing paws. Is he waiting for me?

…

I kiss your hands in devotion.

Your Boccioni

The second letter, probably written on the eve of his departure, bursts with joy, expectation and affection—in it, Boccioni refers to something said by Vittoria in a phone call or written by her in a telegram or letter that has been lost:

Dearest Princess!
The 'dead hen' is strong enough to return to the green hen house on the sweet island! …

I confess I'm not too keen on the name … A Futurist deserved at least to be called a 'dying rooster' but I understand perfectly well that far from the Capitoline Hill, even a Roman princess, in the middle of an argument with the professor of agronomy or a supremely botanical difference of opinion with the gardener, could not humanly have found something better …

Never mind …

The fact is, I wasn't very keen on 'dead hen'!
Then, to remain in character, I said Romanly to myself: It's better to
stop it! Nothing botanical in this, I swear. I'm snubbing the hen house!

In a way, it is a letter like this, even more than those which are more clearly love letters, that allows us to invade (almost indiscreetly, indecently) the privacy of two friends who were also lovers. The humorous expressions, the allusions to shared events, the almost coded language, all suggest that there was now a deep intimacy between Vittoria Colonna and Umberto Boccioni, which involved teasing, intimate memories, and familiar, almost domestic words and gestures.

Vittoria must have told him a lot about herself and her own past, because Boccioni alludes humorously to two famous 'suitors': "The Aga Khan, head of all the Muslims in the Indies, gave you dogs and coffins full of orchids ... I shall allow myself to take to the island a bottle of baked nut oil and a brush ... Isn't that original? It'll be useful to grease Vittoria's gate ... The Kronprinz (may God grant me a sip of water in hell for this) offered you a rose Prussianly hidden in his helmet ... I will take you my book which I hope won't force you to go to bed an hour earlier than usual ... In short, I'm doing what I can and in all sincerity! ... "

On Saturday evening, the eve of his departure, Boccioni wrote his friend Vico Baer what amounted to a confession: "Tomorrow morning, the sixteenth, I am leaving for Pallanza. I will again be a guest of the Princess of Teano who is showing me a kindness which moves me." And he adds: "This new call to arms is a kind of injury ... Never mind!"

Of their second week of love on the Isolino, few traces remain.

What is certain is that, during those days, Vittoria did something which—given the many hundreds of letters sent to her husband during their twenty-year marriage—was quite unique—she practically broke off all contact with Leone. In all the time Umberto Boccioni was staying with her, she would write only a single brief letter. It was as if this new, unexpected and gratifying relationship had succeeded, in a few days, in dealing a blow to a state of affairs that had seemed immutable, supported as it was by a closely woven web of small daily rituals and a superficial but continuous flow of communication. This sudden silence, on the part of a woman who usually wrote to her husband once a day, must surely have aroused Leone's suspicions—or at least taken him by surprise.

In the trunk, among Vittoria's and Boccioni's letters, there are a number of black and white photographs of her on the Isolino. The dates written on them in pen reveal that they were taken during the artist's last stay. They may even have been taken by him, since we know that he was hoping to do a portrait of Vittoria on her island ("he would like to paint us," Vittoria had written to her husband in June, referring to herself and her son, "and I am encouraging him, wondering what on earth will come out") and these photographs may have been a first step.

What do these images tell us of the seven days that Vittoria and Umberto spent together? Just a few details, ultimately— that the weather on the lake was sunny but not too warm (below her skirt Vittoria is wearing silk stockings and light-coloured leather shoes with laces), that the garden was extremely well tended and that the hydrangeas were in full bloom, that the dog, Max, was almost always at the princess's side, and that, despite the melancholy, pensive expression on her face, she always made sure she was well turned out (in the photographs she wears a light-coloured skirt which reveals slim, shapely ankles and a shirt of white organdie with dark trimmings, and on her head she has an elegant straw hat).

Boccioni's letters reveal, even if extremely discreetly, a state of mind very close to bliss: "Here everything is going very well," he writes to his mother, "I am even happier than before. My stay here is magnificent. I am happy." To his friend Vico Baer, he writes: "Every day I go on excursions by automobile and see things I have never seen." He and Vittoria visited Lake Orta and the hermitage of Santa Caterina del Sasso, built on a rock overhanging Lake Maggiore. They had lunch under the shaded pergolas of Isola dei Pescatori and drank white wine. Boccioni had told Vittoria that he had been taken to task by his friends for not yet having visited Isola Bella, and during this last stay he would remedy the omission.

"I was at the Borromeos' yesterday," Vittoria would write to him when he was stationed in Verona, "and I saw again part of those great drawing rooms that we visited together that day: it was better then, wasn't it? … It was one of our most beautiful excursions, but actually everything was beautiful, wasn't it, dear friend? Do you have memories of pleasant days? No one can take those memories from us now, whatever happens."

Boccioni's last stay on the Isolino ended on the twenty-third of July. In Milan, he would barely have time to see one or two friends. Among them was the painter Carlo Carrà, who would recall their last encounter years later in his memoirs. "I see him there, on the street in July 1916 on the edge of a little island of electric light, broad shadows all around him, in the immensity of the night. He talked to me about the first hours of our brotherhood, when in the evening, having finished our work, our souls would meet in aesthetic problems. We both felt that we had been tormenting ourselves too much recently—and we would have liked to unburden ourselves of all the tender feelings that were filling us with emotion on the eve of his departure for Verona, and for death."

It seems likely that Boccioni wrote to Vittoria as soon as he arrived in Milan, but this letter is unfortunately lost. What we have is her reply, dated the twenty-sixth of July.

Dear friend,

Thank you for your beautiful letter which I reread many times. I am moved by the true affection it demonstrates and the words of sincere friendship you found for me. Who knows if in those two weeks we did not create the beginning of something great: a spiritual union from which something will come that will *last: who knows! who knows! Anything may happen, in this case there is the material and there is even a lot of it, what with your great talent and what I can do to encourage you and to make the sincerity of your art known to everyone.*

For now everything is postponed, who knows for how many months …
You have to be a soldier, like everyone, and I'm sure that you will do it very well, in fact! And afterwards, we will come to an agreement for our *war.*

Today you are in Verona and I suppose you will have started your military life which will be even more painful in the early days. What a contrast after the peace and freshness of the Isolino! Here, everything is still as you left it. I pick my flowers, and arrange them in vases. Max sleeps on the veranda, sometimes O and I get him to swim in the lake; in the evening I stay outside until night falls, then I transport myself to my usual corner on the sofa, embroider a little, look at the newspaper, and at ten I turn out the lamp and go up the little staircase to my bedroom. Can you see from this that peaceful and monotonous life, which I have resumed as before, after those two weeks which created a kind of radiant interlude in so much calm? Those two weeks in which we talked about so many beautiful things, and during which you taught me so much.

…

I am ending my letter so that I can post it immediately. I will write often, but I wouldn't like the frequency of my letters to arouse comments here, seeing that I do not have the possibility of posting them myself.

To you, my two Creole *hands!*
Vittoria Colonna.

Umberto Boccioni presented himself at the Verona barracks on Tuesday the twenty-fifth of July at ten-thirty in the evening. That night he slept at the house of his sister Amelia and her husband. Verona surprised him because of "a darkness that's impossible to describe", which made Milan, in comparison, seem like a ballroom.

The following morning he rose early, at five, and by seven was already at the barracks. After a brief roll call, he and his brothers-in-arms, some twenty in all, were left to their own devices in the sun-baked courtyards. In the boredom of that long wait, more than eight hours spent doing nothing, Boccioni walked about, observing.

I talk to a few people then I puff and think. I gave long lessons in drawing to an artilleryman from Frosinone who was drying in the sun two drawings that he had fixed with milk. He was surprised by what I told him. I think he is illiterate but he certainly has ... an aesthetic soul. In conclusion, he told me he couldn't understand why "the government doesn't keep men of education at home because they do honour to the nation ... "

...

I am writing these little details my sweet and good Princess because I know they interest you. If you like I'll write about them often. Tell me if I can write to you in all privacy. Are the addresses all right?

In the middle of the afternoon, Boccioni managed to take refuge in a remote corner of the barracks canteen to write a few letters. The first was to Vittoria. It was written in pencil on green lined paper.

Last night I was in a car, in the dark city, looking at the stars which seemed very white. I thought of them over the calm lake, on the beautiful veranda and I saw the windows of your bright room. Life is very strange and its mechanism illogical ...

As soon as I am settled I will write to the Marchesa di Casanova and Colonel Talamo.

The first letter is for you, my beautiful memory, my radiant hope. If you write to me a good and beautiful and sincere letter in the way that you know, I will be happy and I will await it as a reward.

I spent the journey from Milan to Verona in the company of a convalescent soldier. A bullet had gone clean through his chest. He was from Terracina and kept making me think of the Roman Campagna. I was moved thinking of the dreams of the Roman Campagna outlined on the Isolino—Cisterna, Sermoneta … Castles and infinite landscapes and excursions very close to my ideal, to my soul!

Will I survive all that is in store for me? I am a little sad, I have a slight headache. These courtyards are burning in the sun and yet everything seems dark. All I can see is the light of the lake and the light of my pure and beautiful friend. Write to Boccioni care of Callegari Lungadige Rubele at 4 p.m. Verona.

I kiss your hand with all the warmth of my soul

Boccioni.

" … Tell me if I can write to you in all privacy"—this was the most urgent question, and Vittoria attempted to answer it at the beginning of her letter of the twenty-eighth of July: " … Just write everything that comes into your head—and your heart. When it's no longer all right I will tell you, for now tell me everything, I am living alone and everything you say will remain between us."

Then she told him (rather as she did with Leone, but in a more tender, intimate and even more cheerful tone) the tiny incidents of her daily life—the ferryman who came back dead drunk, the visits, a certain infantry officer to whom she talked about Boccioni … She had been to see the Borromeos again, she also told him, and reminded him of the time when they were together, concluding:

Vittoria during a visit to Leone in the trenches, near the border with Austria (1915).

Sometimes this friendship of ours, which is so complete, seems to me like a dream, which came to illumine my solitary, monotonous life. I often think of it: it was the last thing I was expecting, to find a friend like you on the Isolino! To begin a beautiful—complete—friendship like ours—in the solitude of this summer of war. I knew that I would be here for a few months, I knew that only old friends would come and see me: never would I have imagined this! It is right to say that banal phrase which anyway is not even true: only the unexpected happens.

For today farewell, my friend, I will write in the morning and I will get the chauffeur who takes O for a walk to post it. Write to me often! Change envelopes and handwriting often, in order not to arouse comments.

My two hands—to you!

Vittoria Colonna.

Another recommendation not lacking in significance: "Change envelopes and handwriting often." With good reason, Vittoria did not want to "arouse comments".

By the twenty-ninth of July, however, when he replied to her, he could not have received this letter, since his letter actually begins with an apology for the quality of the paper:

Dearest one!

Forgive the … soldierly paper again … I have not yet gone to Verona. I will go on Monday. Life continues the same. I'm getting used to it, I'm gaining strength and I'm proud of this constant daily sacrifice of everything!

Only someone who lives this life can understand what it is like! Come on! Not a minute goes by when I do not think with a pang in my heart about the sweet Isolino and the dream of days gone by. The city may perhaps help, by being different, and may make me forget a few details. But this constant life in the countryside, in the open air, these meadows, these hills, the clouds, the streams, everything connects me terribly to the days gone by. I'm not sad; rather I have a certain calm sweetness and a soft melancholy. As long as there are exercises, my attention is somewhat distracted. The comical responses of some of my peasant companions and the cruel ignorance of the drill sergeants and corporals distract and divert me. But when I march, in absolute silence, along the white road with these mature, colossal men, with the measured and heavy rhythm of the artillery and the jingling of the spurs, each person's thoughts can be felt flying far away. I see in the huge brown necks of the men in front of me the memory of their families, their villages, their girlfriends ... Then I too, at the rhythm of the marching column, submit to the sweet thoughts that overwhelm me and clutch me and move me. I feel all my sacrifice and reflect that destiny can't take away from me when I return, if I return, the sweet face and dear friend who restored joy, enthusiasm and faith in life to me during that enchanted stay.

I get up at five and have to walk two hundred metres or more to the Adige to wash myself. The noise of the water, the coolness brought by the current, the trees with their immersed trunks, the stones, everything speaks to me of the lake, of the beach on the Isolino, of Max ... By six we are already on the parade ground of an abandoned fortress and we exercise until ten-thirty ...

I think about your breakfast on the terrace. Goethe (?) comes and wakes you up; your big eyes look at the lake, your divine very sweet smile glitters ... And I continue ... one, two ... one, two ... At ten-thirty we go back. My dear friend has already talked to the gardener, perhaps she is arranging flowers in the glass vases ... The big owl glasses, as Onorato calls them, give her face a hint of soft [crossed out: serenity] (I made a mistake, severity) which fills me with awe. Do you remember my tremendous awe? I still feel it and the intimacy of our friendship seems to me to have acquired more value. As I write people around me are laughing and singing and talking. These huge boys forget and are cheerful. I've already set eyes on my orderly, a big peasant with blue eyes, huge red ears and a smile like a delightful little monkey. At eleven, mess rations, which are passable; sometimes I eat sometimes I don't ...

At midday when my Princess passes majestically into the dining room or lingers on the veranda to write a letter or ply her needle I go to my straw mattress to rest. There are thirteen of us ... in a small room in a requisitioned peasant house. At two I go back to the Adige to wash myself, and at two-thirty we fall into line again ... My beautiful friend has lain down on the veranda and is dozing ... May her sleep be a dream as golden and pure as her sweet soul ... Onorato is also lying down reading the Daily Mail ... All this remembering overwhelms me so much it makes me lose the strength to write. Carry on! From two-thirty to five-thirty, exercises. Today, smallpox injections ... At five-thirty when my love has had or is having tea, I, poor soul, go to get my rations ... which sometimes I don't have and I go to a tavern where I find a little chicken and salad. I haven't found anything else since I've been here.

Here, too, the taverns have pergolas which remind me of long, affectionate and chaste talks such as my hunger for love had never before known. Orta and the island and the Isola dei Pescatori, Santa Caterina del Sasso ... After dinner I am free until nine and at nine-thirty I go to bed. And here I think that perhaps I coincide with the life of the Isolino as the beautiful sleepy Princess also goes to bed.

Forgive this slipshod writing of mine my friend. It is impossible to concentrate more than that here. I write as it comes out of me, not as I would like. I don't know when I will be able to put my thoughts in order in this rowdy and promiscuous life. Today we were instructed on the use of the Krupp 75 field cannon. Tomorrow the horses are arriving. You ask me for these details and I'm giving them to you. I haven't received a word in the post. Write to me, I beg you!

29th field artillery
Fifth section, fifth squadron
Verona

At the bottom of the page, in tiny characters, he adds:

I have sent you an address with the first squadron. They've changed me, but I will receive it just the same if you've already written. Please give Onorato a kiss from me. Say hello to the Garden of Victory from me and love me a little. I kiss your hands in all humility!!! Your Boccioni.

And again, at the bottom of the penultimate page, in very small characters and upside down:

I'll write again. Either because of tiredness or the noise I can't give shape to my thoughts which are infinite!! Farewell!!!

Although it is clearly true that Boccioni writes as it "comes out" of him, it is also true that this flow of words, however 'slapdash', has an undeniable communicative force—whether in juxtaposing the "rowdy and promiscuous reality" of Boccioni's life as a soldier with the memory, increasingly idealised as the days passed, of his enchanted time on the Isolino; or in the brief notations on his comrades (peasants sent to fight in the First World War) "mature, colossal men", with "huge brown necks", simple people, mostly illiterate, with whom Boccioni felt a warm, instinctive sympathy, whereas he could not help but find intolerable "the cruel ignorance of the drill sergeants and corporals"; or, finally, in the lyrical, emotional evocation of the "sweet thoughts that overwhelm me and clutch me and move me": the image of her (it is in this letter that he refers to Vittoria for the first time as his "darling") either writing or resting while "your big eyes look at the lake, your divine very sweet smile glitters … "

Vittoria could not help but be profoundly moved, and her emotion is easy to detect even behind the chatty tone with which she recounts visits and outings with her friends and relatives.

Dear friend,
Your letters give me pleasure and pain at the same time, because although you do not really complain, it is obvious how hard your life must be. Hard in every way, not only because of the effort and discomfort, but because of what you must be suffering morally; the forced idleness of your work, in this year of your life when you should be most active—the wasted time which will never return, the separation from the people you love …

*I understand everything you must be feeling so well, and often a wave
of tenderness comes over me thinking of you, I would like to be able to
console you, to be near you a little. I approve of everything you have done:
no one would have had more of an excuse than you to shirk your duty,
but you could not do it because you are you, therefore an act of that kind
would not be possible for you. Dear friend! If you were not like that I
would not be your friend; in those few days when we got to know each
other I sensed your character, I understood immediately that you were
incapable of an act that was—I won't say vile—but something more
common.* Spineless, *let's say. I am* sure *you'll always do the thing that*
needs *to be done, in all circumstances, and I will be much prouder of my*
soldier *friend than of all the others. Keep writing a lot, a lot, giving me
all the details of your life, of the other artilleryman etc. You don't tell me
anything about your nights. How many of you have to sleep together in
the same room? Is everything very dirty? You will think of the blue lake,
and your swims here … I don't imagine there could be a greater contrast:
those days on the Isolino and your life now!—Yesterday was a week since
you left here: have you thought of that? I have. And Saturday was a week
since our last excursion, to Santa Caterina Del Sasso.*

*Yesterday someone called Lieutenant Buzzi came to see me from
Milan—an acquaintance from Rome from the times of the tango—and a
friend of his who I did not know but who asked to drive: I think his name
was Bricherario. They arrived at eleven: after lunch, the usual small
talk, photographs in the garden (if they send them to me you will have
them), Max swimming, etc. Then I took them to have tea on Isola dei
Pescatori in that little restaurant where we had dinner the first evening,
do you remember? They were delighted and made plans to return and
take me to dinner there in the moonlight. I was a little sad to see those
places again, thinking of our beautiful excursions which weren't all at all*
banal *and those two officers, good sorts, poor devils, tired me terribly.
Then we went to Isola Bella, and I saw again all those vast rooms, as
cool as churches, the huge cariatids; the gigantic blue and gold* noeuds
d'amour; *Napoleon's bed, the Queen of England's bed … Then the
garden, the sensitive plant, the white peacocks …*

...

When I got back to the Isolino, I disembarked on the side of 'the Signora's garden' and I felt so weary and languid that I went up to my room and went straight to bed. I had dinner in bed and then I read until late at night. In my book I had put your last two letters and I read them again several times before falling asleep. Dear friend!

We were lucky during those days you were here, that we were completely undisturbed. Now it's as if the word has gone out that it's all right for everyone to come and see me. The day before yesterday it was the turn of a group of acquaintances from Rome who arrived from the Mottorone.

Today the Tyrwhitts are coming from Switzerland and Peppino Compagna from Milan, in the afternoon. I've been to see if their rooms were ready; I feel as if the green one ought to be yours from now on and it hurts me to have to put someone else there. The day after tomorrow, my father-in-law is coming for two days, and the little house will be full. That's my news!

It's starting to get really hot, but on the Isolino there's still air. I'm busy with the garden, I go around with my basket early in the morning. I've now finished putting all fresh flowers in the drawing room—I wish you could see it, it's like a public holiday! How I would love to send you some, but they would all arrive dead, in this heat.

...

All my affection and friendship, dear friend.
Vittoria Colonna

Vittoria wrote this letter on the thirty-first of July, and she must have waited in vain for a reply from Boccioni, since on 4th August she wrote to him: "My friend. It is some days since I last had a letter from you, and I miss it. It may be that you're overwhelmed with work; or perhaps you didn't receive my letter and became discouraged? I hope not. I've written often, and I would have written even more if it were possible for me to post them more easily. I hope to hear from you today."

Then, after recounting more details of what she called her "little life", she announced that a letter of his had arrived in the second post.

Dear one, what can I say? … Every letter moves me greatly, because I see how profound and sincere your feelings for me are. The things you say you could not think and find if they were not true, I feel their spontaneity and am moved by it. I fear that you love me too much, that you will suffer because of it: what if one day you were to hate me? … But no—there is too much understanding between us, too much sympathy, I think we'll always understand each other, won't we?

I have talked about you a lot, these past days, sometimes too much I fear, but it happens quite spontaneously that I'll say 'I came here the other day with B' or things like that. And then often I have spoken on purpose, because I wanted to lay the foundation (is that what they say?) I mean, for everyone to know how serious your art and your personal worth is. These friends of mine are all people who could be useful to you. I'm thinking a lot of the future—I'm meditating on what to do. I want to be useful, *it seems to me that that's the least I can do in return for your great tenderness. You've tried to put me on a pedestal: perhaps you're wrong. I'm a woman like many others, to whom life has given everything* good *but not the* best *of what it could give, looking for that* best *I have lost my way but a certain common sense and the power to judge things calmly has always allowed me to find my way again and regain my balance. I wonder if I've found—or if at least I'm on the track of—something of that mysterious* best *that could make my life complete? After having been all over Europe, met so many people, to find it at last when I'd stopped thinking about it, and actually on the Isolino! … We'll see later: for the moment, I wait and dream. Don't idealise me too much, my friend, but love me. The thought that there is a loyal soul who thinks of me does me good. I think of you often: don't have any doubts knowing that I am no longer alone—there is not a hint of flirtation or* coquetterie *in these friendships of mine—and they also help me to remember with nostalgia the company of another person …*

And she concluded with a piece of advice which—in the light of what would happen in the very near future—sounds eerily like a premonition: "Be careful of the horses kicking: they also kick out to the side, remember. And the bad ones also bite. If you have your own horse—always the same—try to be affectionate to it—it will be much easier to manage."

On the sixth of August Vittoria wrote again to Boccioni, making reference to "two lovely letters" of his, which are unfortunately lost.

What could her lover have written to her? Again we can only speculate. He may have told her more about his brothers-in-arms; he may have talked to her about that longed-for future in which, as she herself wrote in the margin of one page, they would do "great things" together; he may have spoken to her, as he often did, about the sacredness of their love.

We do not know—all we have is the letter that Vittoria wrote to him on the sixth of August.

Dear friend,

Yesterday's posts brought two lovely letters. Believe me, my dear, I very much appreciate all the beautiful things you tell me even though I cannot reply in the same way. The gift you make me of all your thoughts and all that is best in you has a great deal of value, and I realise that. What will come out in the future we do not know: I hope something beautiful, noble and useful. For the moment ... let us wait.

You would not have recognised the Isolino these last few days, there has been such an invasion of friends. I think how extraordinarily *lucky we were during those two weeks not to have a single interruption.*

And here, as she always did, she tells him about the friends who had come to see her, their teas, their days in the garden. But when she recounts their excursion to Orta, she cannot help stopping to recall: "I *thought of the far-away soldier* and the same excursion we took together. What strange days they were! ... Sometimes I wonder if I dreamt them—it was all so unexpected."

At this point she breaks off, and resumes the following day, the seventh of August.

She tells him about her days in the smallest details, even at the cost of seeming "*absurd*", she writes, because it is the only way not to feel their separation too strongly, not to lose contact. Among many other things, Vittoria tells him she received a "very comical" postcard from Giacomo Balla: a postcard which had, perhaps by error, found its way to her mother-in-law, Duchess Ada Caetani, who had not reached Lake Maggiore until the twenty-third of July, the very day Boccioni had left the island. The Duchess, says Vittoria, amused, "forwarded it with a somewhat frosty letter! The postcard is covered in small pieces of paper of every shape and colour with 'Vittoria' written here and there." This object would certainly have increased Leone's mother's suspicions about her daughter-in-law, which was that she was a terribly "fast" woman, as she put it, in other words, of easy virtue.

Vittoria and the friends who were staying with her on the Isolino at the time found the whole thing quite hilarious: "Peppino had such a *fou rire* at the thought that this postcard had ended up in the hands of the duchess that he couldn't stop laughing for ten minutes ... "

The tone, as always, is guarded but affectionate ("Affectionately, Vittoria Colonna", she signed the letter). Vittoria was afraid. She may well have heard that rumours about her and Boccioni were circulating on the shores of the lake. After the lack of caution shown during his last stay on the Isolino, she decided to restore a semblance of order to her life and her marriage. She knew how devastating a scandal could be—she had experienced one at first hand when she was a child. And, with her husband away at the front, such a scandal would have been particularly shameful.

Vittoria's letter to Boccioni ends with the promise that she will write to him as soon as possible. But, mysteriously, Boccioni would receive nothing more from her.

On 7th August, the same day on which Vittoria finished the letter she had begun the previous day, Umberto Boccioni wrote her the most passionate of his letters, in which he recapped the initial phases of their love. If there could still have remained any doubt, in reading their letters, about the true nature of their relationship, they are completely dispelled by the unequivocal passion of this letter, in which, for the first and the only time, he uses the familiar form of address—*tu*—instead of the more formal *voi* and consistently calls her "darling".

He begins by mentioning the last letter he had received from her (the one written on the fourth of August):

It's the most beautiful, darling! It's the best even more than the other ones: all beautiful and good! Why should I hate you? Why should I idealise you too much? What there is between us is a profound reality, it was born as reality. However recently we had met, and become friends ... there is our secret, that wonderful crescendo which led us from chastity to chastity to our chaste pleasure! O, our nights! Your pallor, your confusion, my terror, our infinite communion of body and spirit. My divine one, I feel that you love me, a little, a little more than when you measured me with avarice with the tip of your little finger ... Do you remember? How I am yours! How I am your brother and friend, how I admire you, always, with every breath, always! Always!

If my letters are delayed, do you miss them a little? Do you desire me a little? I've never been so humble with a woman! Is that good? Is it bad? I am yours, this I know, and I feel that every day this infinite devotion of mine grows.

Darling, don't be sad if I have to find out that you go all over again with others on the excursions that belong to us ... What can we do? That's life. That's how it is! I want you to continue your life, naturally, I'm content as long as when others see you lost in thought, your thought is

Vittoria, probably photographed by Boccioni, beside one of the huge hydrangea bushes she herself had planted (July 1916).

me. I'm overflowing with love for you here! Last night when I went to bed I caught myself biting my handkerchief and whispering your name. What would become of me under the burden of this heavy, solitary life if I were not sustained and uplifted by the fresh softness of your memory. To me you are a purpose and a hope. And I thank you! You fill my spirit the way religious people feel full of the spirit of God. I don't know when my brain will start working. This life makes it seem very heavy. Do you think I would write to you like this from my studio? But you are a woman who can push me to heights one dares not hope for. Here, though, my heart lives only because of you, my beauty, my sweet child. Do you know that you inspire me like a child, and fill me with awe like a mother? You are everything to me, darling! my darling! Let me say it! Thank you for having made me realise that I am a little dear to you and that you think of me. Write to me again, always, always more! You know that yesterday, I had just read a few lines of your good letter when the sergeant gave me the duties of a corporal ... and took me out of the ranks and put me in command of my own squadron of twenty men? As you see, my career is a rapid one. I don't yet have the rank on my arm because I must have my training as a soldier and then as a learner-corporal. That will come later. I am a corporal in pectore *... I had to put your letter in my pocket in a hurry and cry attention! forward! march!!! ... Imagine how confused I was ... Commanding is not easy. You need a sharp, strong, authoritarian voice. I will do it! ... What do you say? You see, you who always called me the town mouse? This morning I rode a horse for the first time. And I was complimented by the second lieutenant because of the nimble way I mounted without using the stirrup. You leap on the horse by hoisting yourself up on your arms with one hand on the neck and one on the saddle. Instead of walking the horse, I trotted it. In that too I was thinking of you and I imagined that I would learn to do a few trots with you. When? Darling!*

On Saturday, while I was rubbing down the horse, a large automobile arrived with two chauffeurs, two second lieutenants, a lieutenant and a captain. What a sensation! My sergeant called me. They were friends I'd met in Verona who had come to pick me up. You can't imagine their laughter when they saw me rubbing down with my stable cap on. They want to photograph me when they come back. They went immediately to my lieutenant, who immediately gave me leave. I had a little wash (my orderly prepares all my non-regulation things until they shine …) and half an hour later I was in Verona. We drove around in the automobile for a while, then went to a café which is like the Cova in Milan.

Those lieutenants were full of women. As for me, my darling, I immediately felt out of place; I smiled and greeted everyone as if in a daze. I even grew a little melancholy. What could all those women do for me when I my heart is full of you?

Boccioni ended by thanking Vittoria for having spoken about him to her friends:

How grateful I am to you! … Tell me about yourself! Tell me about us, about our future. Darling you have given me a tremendous love for life! I want to go back! I want to see you again and adore you, as much as you want! Aren't I good? Farewell! Farewell. Write to me. I kiss you all over with all my ardour and my tenderness. Send me a kiss, my darling! Yours,

U. Boccioni.

Before ending, he added a postscript.

I'm sending you these two photographs which were taken five minutes after my … enrobing by my friend the lawyer Piccoli who came from Milan to see me. They seem to me pretty and very fine as photographs. Write and tell me if you really like them. If you don't, throw them away. You make me strangely afraid my darling. Why? Everything seems unworthy of you. How many things I have to tell you. Write to me. Now that you don't use your* *paper write to me as you did when you spoke to me. Darling, abandon yourself as you did on those evenings. Don't you feel me at your feet loyal and loving?*

I kiss your large beautiful eyes

your B.

* Underlined twice.

From the time he wrote this letter, Boccioni was to hear nothing more from Vittoria. On the fifteenth of August, after a gap of eight days, Boccioni sent Vittoria a short, anxious letter. It was written in black ink on blue-grey paper and lacks an envelope. Perhaps (like the previous one) it was sent through a friend. The letter—written the day before his fatal fall—begins with a formal "Dear Princess", as if to apologise for the passionate tone of his previous letter. Boccioni says that he is surprised not to have heard from her: "Are you ill perhaps?" he asks. "What's happened? Have you completely forgotten me? I don't understand!" And he ends: "I hope to receive a line which will set my mind at rest … " Her long silence had worried him. It made him imagine the most terrible things that might have prevented her from writing. More than anything else, probably, he feared that his previous letter, in which he had revealed how intimate their relationship had become, had been intercepted and had ended up, like Balla's postcard, in the hands of the Duchess of Sermoneta—or even in those of Leone.

During this solitary wait, Umberto Boccioni tried to distract himself by riding. To his friends he confessed that he wanted to learn for the day when he would be able to accompany Vittoria to the Pontine Plain. They had talked about it, in their hours of intimacy, and she had promised him that, once the war was over, she would take him to explore Fogliano, Sermoneta, Ninfa …

Like many members of the high aristocracy, Vittoria was a skilful rider. She had learnt to ride as a child, this being part of what was considered a 'good upbringing'. Even Onorato had been forced to take riding lessons as a child. "It does him good," Vittoria had written to Leone, "and besides it would be a shame later if he didn't know how to ride."

Umberto, on the other hand, had never learnt to ride. But now that life in the regiment offered him the opportunity to ride every day, he took full advantage of it. "I ride a lot," he wrote to her, with a certain pride, on the fifteenth of August, "until I'm exhausted. Yesterday evening I did ten kilometres. This morning I've been on horseback all the time. I like it and I'm making progress."

On the sixteenth of August, Umberto Boccioni wrote what was, in all probability, the last letter of his life: in one go, on a sheet folded in four. It was addressed to Vittoria.

Dear friend,

I waited today too for the post and didn't receive anything. I can't understand it! Are you ill? Does it bore you to reply? Have my letters bored you? What's happened? I don't understand! I live in a state of excitement that won't give me any peace. I don't even have the strength to ride a horse. In what way have I failed? Of what am I guilty? Is it possible that such a pure friendship can be cut short like this without a word? I don't understand …
I ask myself a thousand questions, I examine my own conduct, I don't find anything, I no longer know what you're thinking about, I live discouraged, without having the strength to do anything. This solitude is terrible!

On the other hand, I don't want to write too often because my attentions towards you might be wrongly interpreted by others. Do you understand me? I've never thought badly of you in all this waiting, I've never doubted you. That's why I can't be content with waiting, I can't find peace, this is a mystery which I cannot explain. Can some letters have got lost? Anyway the time that has passed is now so long that a second letter must be overdue.

I hope nothing bad has happened to you. I wait with confidence and wish you every happiness.

I am still your very devoted friend

Boccioni

29th field artillery
Fifth section, fifth squadron
Verona

"I don't even have the strength to ride a horse": in the light of what was to happen a few hours later, this phrase, too, has a particularly sinister ring. The postmark on the envelope indicates that the letter was sent on the sixteenth of August 1916. By the time it arrived on the Isolino, two days later, he was already dead.

The fact was that, during all that time, Vittoria had never stopped writing to Boccioni. On the seventeenth of August, surprised that he had not heard from her, she wrote: "I don't feel I've been so silent—perhaps there has been some delay in the post, or one of my letters has been mislaid? In short, by now you really must have heard from me, and you will have realised that there is *no change* or upset in my life."

It was still the same little life, she repeated. The only difference was that it was raining; and this reminded her of her summers in England, the balls, the bicycle races, her flirtations with "young men".

"It's been years since I last thought about these things, but this long day of rain has brought these memories back. I would love those times to return. Why can't we live twice? But I can't complain, it's stupid to say that."

After which she told him at length about her plans. She would go to Viareggio, "to see again that *bande* from Rome"; then back to the Isolino; then, perhaps, winter in Rome, although that was not certain, perhaps the house would not be open (there were no servants!), and she would go and stay at the Grand Hotel … From her tone, it seems that the princess was once again every inch a princess. There may have been a reason for this: Vittoria feared that these lines might be seen by prying eyes.

This letter, in fact, contains a valuable piece of information, the one clue we have as to the mystery of the disappearing letters. Lately she had given all her letters to Onorato's new tutor, "a bearded gentleman … who, I suspect, is not overly fond of soap and water." This gentleman was a local schoolmaster who, apart from tending to the needs of Onorato, was given the task of going to Intra every day to post and collect the mail. Realising that some of her letters had not reached their destination, Vittoria must have had her suspicions. That day, she wrote to Boccioni, she decided to go and post the letter herself. And indeed it would arrive at its destination, but too late. On the white envelope which still contains it we find the words: *Arrived after his death.* Of the other letters written by her during the last week of Boccioni's life and given to Onorato Caetani's new tutor, all trace has been lost.

Where did Vittoria's last letters to Umberto Boccioni end up? Did the new tutor get rid of them or did he give them to someone in the Caetani household, the duchess perhaps, or even Leone?

That is, of course, possible. At the time Ada, the duchess of Sermoneta, was staying with her husband near Lake Maggiore, where she had many friends. These friends may well have brought her up to date with the gossip about that summer relationship on the Isolino. Ada detested Vittoria and it is quite possible that, wanting to find out how true the gossip was and to protect her eldest son Leone and all the family from possible scandal, she made efforts to find out more. Onorato's new tutor, who, as we discover from Vittoria's letters, apart from not doing much work was also a person of weak character—spineless, in fact—who was always short of money, was an ideal accomplice. In addition, Onorato's tutors were paid by the Caetani administration, which meant that they were directly dependent, not on Vittoria, but on Leone's parents, the Duke and Duchess of Sermoneta.

Obviously, it is not certain that this is what happened. It might have been the military censors, known to have been very active at that time, who stemmed the flow of this amorous correspondence.

"There is an animal," Vittoria would write to Leone some months after Boccioni's death, "who opens all my letters—it may be some malingering servant who knows us and is curious to know all our business, because the servants' letters, for example, are never opened and mine always are … " Opened or closed, though, sooner or later the letters reached their destination, while those sent by Vittoria to Boccioni through the tutor seem to have vanished into thin air.

In Vittoria Colonna's rediscovered correspondence there is also a long letter from Emilio Piccoli (Boccioni's lawyer friend) describing the last days and hours of the artist's life. It is dated the first of September 1916, and is tied together with Vittoria's letters to Boccioni, which Piccoli himself had retrieved at her request.

On his arrival at Sorte, Boccioni had "demonstrated a great passion" for riding. "On his first day in the saddle," writes Piccoli, "he was as happy as a young boy," and everyone had admired his "amazed enthusiasm for the new training".

Boccioni had chosen an elegant horse for himself, light almond in colour, and five or six years old. The animal was "good and well-tamed, and he would certainly have won it over with caresses and pieces of sugar." This love for animals (shared by Vittoria) was characteristic of Boccioni. At twenty-four, having experienced "the obscene sight of butcher's meat", he had copied into his diary a quotation from Leonardo da Vinci: "A time will come when people will be content, like me, with a diet of vegetables and the killing of animals will be considered on a par with murder." For a time he even became a vegetarian. Emilio Piccoli, in his letter, recalls how his friend loved to touch "a horse's *muzzle* (as he called it)" and stroke its rump. Seeing them fall, as they often did, "shocked him and made him really upset", and, if a coachman beat "his exhausted nag with a stick", Boccioni "would get out of his coach and dismiss him harshly".

On his first day in the saddle, Boccioni did a good seventeen kilometres and, despite the fact that his knees were bleeding, he would have continued if the sergeant had not ordered him to turn back.

"Of his enthusiastic tenacity," Piccoli writes with a sentimentality that would have annoyed Boccioni, "what strikes me, more than the sense of duty, was his firm intention to learn in the shortest possible time the elegant art of riding since he was still one of those who dream of rides along the seashore, in the full moon, and sighs of love whispered on the thresholds of castles. He certainly had hopes of preparing himself for rides in the Roman Campagna, with which you had perhaps amiably detained him, inviting him for after the war, and I understand his dream so divinely entertained."

At seven-thirty in the evening on Wednesday the sixteenth of August, a few hours after sending Vittoria his last letter, Boccioni asked permission to go riding again. His sergeant granted permission and even decided to go with him. They left their barracks side by side and rode for about four hundred metres outside the village of Sorte then turned and rode back quickly.

At a bend, Boccioni's horse reared and set off at a gallop along the road from which they had just come. Boccioni lost his balance and tried to grab hold of the animal's neck while the sergeant, surprised by the abrupt movement, rushed to his aid, but to no avail. Boccioni, according to this reconstruction, had fallen head first and lay injured in the middle of the road. The sergeant dismounted, lifted him and called for help. At that moment a military van arrived. A straw mattress and a blanket were placed on the ground and the wounded man was laid on them, his head and shoulders still in the sergeant's arms. At that point, Boccioni still had "his eyes open and alert" and he responded with a look "to the loving words of his superior" who, Piccoli would write to Vittoria, was certain that "his pulse had been perfectly regular as far as the gates of Verona."

When they got to the hospital in Verona, the wounded man was handed over to the doctor on duty, who immediately realised that the case was hopeless. Two hours later, Boccioni's lieutenant arrived, gave him a caffeine injection, and tried to speak to him. He asked if he had fallen from his horse, Emilio Piccoli recounts, "to which Umberto replied no, with a nod of his head and with his voice.

"Then the lieutenant said, 'Boccioni, do you recognise me?' And he replied, 'Yes, you are my lieutenant.'

"'But then,' the lieutenant insisted, 'you fell from your horse.' The dying man again said, 'No.' It was the last word he uttered."

It is hard to imagine the reason, if there was any, for this repeated denial. Years earlier, in his diary, Boccioni had written a sentence which, in the light of his death, assumes a strange significance: "I believe in love as an absolute idea which is integrated with a leap into the infinite." It was almost as if ideal, absolute love was incompatible with daily life. "It is clear," he continued on the same page, "that for opposites which try to achieve absolute love to become integrated, being two bodies in constant transformation, they must resign themselves to achieve it and perish or survive miserably as do all those unable in any way to duplicate absolute integration."

In other words, love and death were indissolubly linked. Could only death—"the leap into the infinite"—save absolute love from being a wretched survival of itself?

Umberto Boccioni died on the seventeenth of August 1916. That same morning Vittoria, unaware of the tragedy that was taking place in Sorte, wrote him the letter in which, as we have seen, she tried to reassure him that there was "*no change*" in her feelings. She also indulged in beautiful memories of when she was a girl and her life was like an open book, yet to be written. And all at once, for the first time, there emerged in her words an impetuous, vital desire—to liberate herself from the aesthetic framework in which she was confined, to have the courage to take life with both hands and be completely happy: "Life has given me a lot—if it has not given me more it may be because I couldn't or wouldn't take it—now I *want* to find *true* happiness—I am searching for it."

That love that had grown by chance on the Isolino seems to become, in Vittoria's words, something indispensable, something very close to happiness. In a letter written about the same time to Leone, who was still unaware of anything, she even confessed: "If it were not for the constant thought of the danger in which you are living, I would say that I've never been as happy as I am now."

But Vittoria did not succeed in savouring such a strong emotion, such a strong hope, for long. Perhaps she feared, or at least suspected, that declaring herself happy might arouse the envy, and therefore the revenge, of the gods. She chose to withdraw into a protective shell of silence and waiting: ultimately, if one thought about it clearly, happiness, she wrote in her last letter to Boccioni, was not something that had to be seized by force but, on the contrary, something that "had to be sustained". It was important to "scrutinise the horizon … and wait a while". It was her old fear speaking, her anxiety that if she allowed the great currents of emotion, the underground river of existence, to come to the surface, the polished, comfortable patina of her life would be cracked irreparably.

Umberto Boccioni would never read that last letter. After his death, the letter she had written him on the sixth of August was found in his wallet: he had put it there to have it with him always.

The day after his death, the artist was temporarily buried in the war cemetery in Verona. Only a few friends were present: his family had not been informed. The field was strewn with

Umberto Boccioni near Verona just a few weeks before his death (July 1916).

thousands of identical stones, each one of which marked a life cut short by the war. For practical reasons, there were no names on the gravestones, only numbers. Umberto Boccioni had been given the number 1003.

Emilio Piccoli described the funeral in his letter to Vittoria Colonna.

We laid flowers (and I thought of you in arranging them) and tried to form a mound to overcome that desolate and flat uniformity and stood there without speaking, I petrified with grief, and almost dazed, thinking it wasn't possible and that He was about to come back to us at any moment, with his open, youthful smile, his strong, loyal voice, with his firm hand held out, a hand that did not betray, with his proud sparkling eyes, the mirror of a mind that was always alert and powerful.

Vittoria learnt about Boccioni's death from the newspapers on the morning of the nineteenth of August.

THE FUTURIST PAINTER BOCCIONI DIES IN A FALL FROM A HORSE

Verona, 18, night. The Futurist painter Boccioni, currently a soldier in the 29th artillery, was riding a horse near Chievo the other evening when the animal suddenly reared and he received a serious wound to the head which proved fatal despite the best efforts of the doctors.

This paragraph was carefully cut out by Vittoria and put with her and Boccioni's letters and with the few photographs from that summer.

On the twenty-second of August, Vittoria Colonna took up pen and paper and wrote to Leone:

My darling,

I haven't written to you for two or three days. I have been very sad about Boccioni's death—he died falling off a horse last Wednesday. I read about it in the newspaper. I couldn't believe it—I had received a letter from him that day. I wanted to go to Verona for the funeral: there was no train for Milan which would allow me to catch the connection to Verona, so I set off by car, ten kilometres from Milan we had a flat tyre, and that put paid to my hopes of taking the train to Verona. I remembered his address in Milan, so I went there instead, which turned out lucky as I found his poor sister alone, dealing with his half-paralysed old mother, whom she did not yet dare tell the truth. I stayed with them all afternoon, then his sister's husband came from Verona and we had to tell his mother the truth. I've never seen such a strong expression of human grief—it was so awful that I will never forget it. This is a woman who was abandoned by her husband years ago, and her son had meant everything to her, he had given her all his earnings, had pulled her out of poverty because before she had had to sew even to maintain her children. Now they lived comfortably in a nice little apartment, and, as she said, at least as an old woman she could start to breathe. I don't think fate has ever done anything as cruel as this. In fact, the old mother, who, while there was still hope had spent the whole long afternoon praying, when she heard that he was dead rose straight up on her crutches and said loudly: God does not exist. She was right. I went back to see them the next morning, and put in his studio, over his paintings and statues, the flowers that I had brought from the Isolino. We arranged his canvases all around: so much work, so much talent. What beautiful things done between the ages of twenty and twenty-six, before he became a Futurist—and even afterwards, works that are incomprehensible but wonderful effects of colour and imagination.

It is a great loss for Italy, more than people think, because he was only at the beginning: *in fact, he always said that life will begin tomorrow, after the war, he had things to do, to do. Full of plans, full of a desire to live, now all over! To me, it is a huge loss, a friendship that was to have given me an interest and satisfaction for my whole life. I am still in a daze.*

I came back here the day before yesterday, there was no point now in going to Verona, the funeral was over, I will go later and lay flowers on his grave. I found here the faithful Visconti who was very good to me. He brought me lunch in bed and kept me company. Then, afraid I was going to spend a sleepless night, I took too much veronal and I felt bad all of yesterday. Now I am better. Visconti has left. I am putting my things in order and tomorrow I will go back to Milan for one night: to see Gelasio and take more flowers to Boccioni's studio. Then I'll carry on to Viareggio, where I will spend ten days with Jane and hope to get over the shock of these days. Death is such a terrifying thing for someone who believes in nothing: where does such a lively intelligence go,* such a formidable joie de vivre, a desire to work, to do, to achieve, all snuffed out like a lamp because a stupid horse started to kick! The bad luck of it! To die. It is basically so difficult to die. We may feel ill, break our nose, break our leg, but to die—what bad luck.

My darling, take care of yourself. I've lost my nerve. I have a kind of feeling that I bring bad luck to anyone who comes close to me. I beg you to be careful. If anything happened to you I don't think I would be able to stand it. From your letters, I can see that the life you are living is terrible. Think of me and be careful. No, don't think of me, because I bring bad luck, forget me, but be careful.

In posthumous exhibitions and catalogues devoted to Umberto Boccioni, like that published in 1988 on the occasion of a major retrospective at the Metropolitan Museum in New York, there are often photographs of his studio in Milan. They were taken after his death. In the white, light-filled rooms, there are dried flowers placed here and there on the tables, the easels, and on the late plaster casts, many of which have been lost. Now it is known that these flowers came from the Isolino, and that it was Vittoria who placed them there in a final gesture of tenderness for her young lover.

*   Underlined twice.

"A soul that bounds. A volcanic sensibility," Marinetti would write recalling Umberto Boccioni. "A brilliant river at full flood, always going all the way, all the way, everything, everything, without half measures, without calculations, for the Futurist renewal of Italy, but also for less: a friend, a cloud ... And then immediately his sharp eyes would escape him delicately in the most graceful humour. To enjoy himself, to love, to destroy in order to create, to fight and to die, but laughing."

Boccioni went through Vittoria Colonna's life like a wave of unpredictable gaiety. "This interlude in our lives", "a radiant interlude": that was how she described their brief unexpected love which had blossomed amid the greenery of the Isolino.

In the days immediately following Boccioni's death, Vittoria took refuge, as she had announced to her husband, in Viareggio, at the house of her great American friend Jane di San Faustino.* The frivolous, carefree atmosphere of the resort exacerbated her grief. "It is the most insipid life there can be, especially in times like these," she wrote to Leone, "and I assure you that I feel ashamed." But it was the only life she knew.

Her friend Carlo Visconti, who, as we have seen, had been Vittoria's guest on the island the day she heard the news of Boccioni's death, would subsequently send her a "consoling" letter. Fate, he would write, had been "prudent" with her because this death had prevented her taking a step that could only have done her harm. This can only mean one thing: that Vittoria had confessed to her "ever-loyal friend", that she had wanted to seize that unexpected happiness. Visconti, who also belonged to the upper echelons of the aristocracy, would have understood, but would certainly not have approved. It was evident, from his letter to Vittoria, that if the relationship between her and the painter had continued, it could only have resulted in failure and unhappiness since "all the realities of the world, of society, of life" stood

---

*   Jane's daughter, Virginia, would marry in 1919 Edoardo Agnelli, son of the Senator Giovanni and founder of Fiat.

between her and that person. The indication was clear: for order to be maintained, at all levels, it was necessary to make a clear distinction between the head and the heart, between one's public role and one's private feelings. "Keep the images, the feelings, the moments, the perfume of that week you told me about," Visconti concludes, "deep, deep in your memory, that they may be evoked for themselves, but never speak of them to anyone. The years will pass and you will return to it as to the most hidden, the dearest, the saddest treasure that existence has left you."

From all appearances, Vittoria followed this advice: with the help of Emilio Piccoli, she recovered the letters she had written to Boccioni, bound them together with those he had sent her and kept them for years, jealously and in silence.

During the 1920s and 1930s, while keeping up a frenetic life of travel and parties, Vittoria wrote a sea of words: books of memoirs, travel articles, society columns. She recounted her life from early childhood to the grim, solitary years of the Second World War. She wrote about her many friends and loved to recall her somewhat bohemian life during the carefree years of the *belle époque*, when artists, writers and intellectuals passing through Rome would come to see her in the small drawing room of Palazzo Caetani. But never a word did she write about Umberto Boccioni.

Two paintings by Boccioni, a portrait of his mother and one of his Futurist dynamisms (probably bought by Vittoria after the artist's death to help his mother) ended up—almost as though she preferred not to have them always in front of her—in the darkness of the loft at Palazzo Orsini.

"I can never forget the Isolino," Vittoria Colonna would write years later in her memoirs, "the hours spent in a boat both by day and night, the moonlight on the water, the bathing from my own beach, the breathless heat of summer and the unbelievably fierce gales that swept down from Mergozzo in the autumns … "*

* In English in the original.

And that is all that the princess would allow herself to remember of that summer of 1916.

Vittoria Colonna would continue to spend her summers on the little island until 1925, just as she would continue to devote herself to her houses, her gardens, and her embroidery. In Rome, when the war was over, she would go and live in Palazzo Orsini, grandly renaming it Palazzo Sermoneta. What most attracted her in this edifice built by Sienese architect Baldassarre Peruzzi on the imposing remains of the theatre of Marcellus was the inner courtyard, an ideal place to create a small, secluded garden. Over the years, Vittoria would fill it with fountains and shrubs, so that in spring its rooms would be pervaded with the cool scent of orange blossom and jasmine.

Some photographs taken at Palazzo Orsini at the beginning of the 1950s show Vittoria in the twilight of her life (she would die in London on the seventh of November 1954). The drawing room of her apartment is filled with seventeenth- and eighteenth-century furniture and ancient Roman busts. Here and there are vases of flowers. Vittoria is still elegant, even though the bright colours of her youth have been replaced with darker shades. Her hair, cut short, is grey. Her long tapering hands are well tended, the nails painted red. Her face, though marked by time, is still beautiful, even though the eyes are enigmatic and distant.

"You will achieve something in this world," she had written years earlier to her husband, "but I will have been a silly pleasure-loving woman who never knew how to do anything in life except love, but did that very well."

Now that the years of love were over for ever, Vittoria's eyes were misty with boredom.

Of Onorato Caetani, Boccioni's "young friend", few traces remain. He lived with his mother and with the few people paid to look after him. He died at the age of forty-five, just after the Second World War. There are still people in Rome who remember his imposing, solitary figure crossing the historical centre with big lopsided steps.

Maestro Ferruccio Busoni was devastated by the death of his young friend. At the end of July 1916, he had written a letter to Boccioni to tell him how much he disapproved of his decision to go back to the front. He particularly deplored the forced interruption of work which at San Remigio, he wrote, "had begun with such fine impetus."

After hearing of his death, Busoni wrote a grief-stricken article about Boccioni which was published on the thirty-first of August 1916, on the front page of the Swiss newspaper the *Neue Zürcher Zeitung*. In it, he attacked the propagandist rhetoric of the Italian newspapers, which simply praised the heroism Boccioni had shown in "wanting at all costs to be a soldier", but did not mention the terrible loss for Italy of such a great artistic talent. Busoni also published an extract from the last letter he had received from Boccioni:

"From this life I will emerge with a kind of defiance of everything which is not art," the artist had written to his friend five days before his death. "Nothing is greater than art. Everything I see is a game compared with the right brushstroke, the right line of verse or chord of music. I want to develop this idea if I have the time and the will. Everything is mechanical and facile and routine. Patience and memory. There is nothing but art with its unknowable breath and its inscrutable depths."

As for Leone Caetani, having spent weeks being made aware, through Vittoria's letters, of Boccioni's presence on the Isolino and in her life, he must surely have heard about the rumours circulating on the shores of the lake and in the drawing rooms of the capital about that love which Vittoria, for a brief but indelible moment, had stopped concealing from the eyes of the world. And it is quite possible that it was reading her letters from the Isolino—especially the last one, written after the artist's death—that made him realise there was no longer any future for them.

In 1916, a few months after the death of Boccioni and one year before himself dying of Spanish flu, Guillaume Apollinaire devoted a poem to his generation—which was also the generation of the first avant-gardes, the Futurists, and Leone and Vittoria—in which, speaking for those young people eternally torn between order and adventure, he asked only one thing of those who would judge them: *Be indulgent.*

Leone Caetani, who, until the summer of 1916, had managed to maintain a semblance of order, suddenly broke free after Boccioni's death, tearing apart the fabric that had previously kept him and Vittoria together. We do not know if this rebellion was caused by his pain at her dramatic betrayal or the emergence, out of the wreckage (of his marriage, and of the war), of a new feeling: a sense of the preciousness of life, and a desire to pursue his own happiness immediately and at whatever cost. Forever torn between order and adventure, Leone—who had always clung to a family history that went back nearly a thousand years and to a marriage which was the final element in that history—now, once and for all, chose adventure.

In August 1917, exactly one year after the death of Umberto Boccioni, Sveva, the daughter of Leone Caetani and Ofelia Fabiani, was born. Vittoria pretended to see nothing, to know nothing. She made plans, imagined situations of domestic harmony, and continued to write tirelessly to her husband. "Our home *must* be set up properly and we *must* live according to the traditions of our caste," she wrote to him from Palazzo Orsini-Sermoneta in 1920. In another letter, written the same year, we read: "In any case I have decided to have a beautiful, well-put-together house such as befits Vittoria Colonna, Duchess

Leone with Ofelia Fabiani and their daughter Sveva just before they left for Canada (c 1921).

of Sermoneta." Instead, Leone (who had inherited the title of duke on his father's death in 1917) built a villa at the top of the Janiculum, the highest of Rome's hills. He called it Villa Miraggio—a five-storey architectural folly topped by a central tower and surrounded by a terraced garden and a high perimeter wall—and went to live there together with Ofelia Fabiani and their daughter. This was a gesture of total defiance, which in Roman high society would be judged unacceptable.

Marginalised by what had been his own world, unable to legitimise his daughter within Italian law as it was then constituted, and increasingly at odds with the political situation in Italy, Leone would leave Rome in 1921 and take refuge in Vernon, British Columbia, where Sveva would finally be able to take her father's name. In 1928 Leone Caetani became a Canadian citizen. He was stripped of his Italian citizenship by the regime in 1935, a few months before his death, which occurred in Vancouver on Christmas Day that same year.

"This is not an abandonment of my country and my affairs," he had written to a woman friend in one of his first letters from Vernon, "but a return to simple nature, to a primitive life, a longing for peace and rest after the torment of war and the post-war period. A spiritual rest … "

Once, when I was just beginning my 'investigation' into Leone Caetani, I set off to find traces of him in Canada. It was an October day, and the air was imbued with the warm breeze and golden hues of an Indian summer. I found a shady garden, bordered with lilies, overlooking a valley of lakes and orchards and a simply furnished house with large windows looking out on the garden and wooden floors.

I climbed up an external staircase which Leone had built with his own hands, which leads to a small square roof terrace. It was here (so a close friend of his daughter told me) that Leone would lie for hours on end on summer evenings, looking up at the sky, in the company of his dogs. In the darkness, surrounded by silence, he would gaze at the stars, which in that part of the world seem very close.

Leone's garden and house displayed a similar, if somewhat more extreme, aesthetic to what Vittoria had created on the Isolino. Once again, it was a sheltered, isolated world, based entirely on an idea of simplicity and naturalness a long way from the burden of history and the baroque splendour of the Roman palaces in whose shadow they had both grown up.

"And so I have become what the English call a 'failure' ... I haven't succeeded in anything," he wrote in a letter sent to his former assistant, Giorgio Levi della Vida, a few months before his death at the age of sixty-six. "Here in Canada, leading a simple life ... I have found a great deal of peace, and above all, concentrating on myself, I have acquired that inestimable good which is serenity of mind, a purely contemplative good, free of ambition and regret, ready to accept with tranquillity anything that fate has in store for me. Is this happiness? I don't know ... "

And what of Ofelia Fabiani? What happened to the graceful girl of the *café chantant*? The valley of the Okanagan was supposed to have been only a long halt, a pause for breath on a road still rich in promise at the side of the Duke of Sermoneta. When she arrived at the tiny station of Vernon, in that distant spring of 1921, the twenty-four-year-old Ofelia had with her an incredible number of trunks. For a while, she and Leone continued to travel: to Mexico, the United States, and Europe. Once, they even returned to Italy, and went to visit the Caetani estates on the Pontine Plain, then nothing more. When Leone died, Ofelia was thirty-eight years old. From that moment she refused all contact with the world, and forced her daughter to do the same. From time to time, overcome with nostalgia, Ofelia would rummage in her trunks and put on one of her magnificent dresses bought years earlier in Paris. Then, elegantly attired and made up, she would go and stand in front of the mirror or parade through the house like a mannequin.

Sveva Caetani and her Danish governess Miss Maria Jüül—who would devote her life to the child she had been entrusted with years earlier—would also spend the rest of their days in Canada. The half-sister of the "Futurist boy", Onorato, so cherished by Boccioni—who would also inherit her father's height—would not have any children. After Ofelia died in 1960, Sveva emerged from the restrictions imposed by her mother and took her first timid steps into the world. She was forty-three years old. Of her father's share of the immense Caetani fortune there remained only the little wooden house and the wooded garden near the blue waters of Lake Kalamalka. She found work in a local school and devoted herself to what had always been her secret passion, fiercely opposed by Ofelia: painting. In the course of her long life, she would become a highly regarded artist in British Columbia. And although her eyes remained firmly fixed on the past—on Rome and the history of the Caetanis—she would experiment with an individual, mould-breaking pictorial language. For years she would try to reconstruct the events that had led her and her family to become uprooted from Rome and the Caetani history and settle, like maple seeds borne on the wind, in this lunar, half-deserted landscape, the preserve of pioneers and wild animals. In the end she would give up the idea of finding an answer, because ultimately—as she herself wrote in a book dedicated to the memory of her father—in life there is nothing to understand, only love.

Before leaving the scene at the age of seventy-seven (she died in Vernon in 1994) Sveva Caetani would transform the little house in the woods and its garden—the final residence of the Duke of Sermoneta—into a cultural centre giving accommodation to young artists.

"The artist is the translator of the chaos that envelops things," Umberto Boccioni had proclaimed in a lecture on Futurist painting in 1911. "We see colours, we hear harmonies, we weep and laugh and hate in life just as artists have shown in art."

This curious coincidence, this passion for art germinating (as if by some strange cross heredity) in the last of the Caetanis would surely have brought the hint of an ironic smile to Boccioni's face.

Vittoria Colonna, Duchess of Sermoneta, in the garden of Palazzo Orsini in Rome, a few months before her death (1954).

A Note on the Text

The Boccioni-Colonna correspondence is preserved in the Fondazione Camillo Caetani and consists of nineteen letters: eleven by Boccioni and eight by Vittoria Colonna, plus a fragment of a letter of hers that was never sent.

Vittoria's neatly handwritten letters are almost all written in pen on blue paper with her monogram in the top left hand corner; Boccioni's are written in pen or pencil on all kinds of sheets of paper—yellow, green, grey, lined and unlined, of various sizes—and are full of deletions. For this book, the letters have been transcribed faithfully in their final versions, and their peculiarities of layout, syntax and punctuation have been preserved.

In addition to the letters of Vittoria Colonna and Umberto Boccioni, the collection also includes the long letter written to Vittoria by the lawyer Emilio Piccoli and another, also to Vittoria, by Carlo Visconti.

Acknowledgements

This book came into being thanks to the support of the Fondazione Camillo Caetani and its president, the lawyer Giacomo Antonelli, to whom I owe a deep debt of gratitude. I would like to thank Caterina Fiorani, present curator of the Caetani archive, while at the same time remembering with gratefulness her late father, Professore Luigi Fiorani who curated the archives for so many years.

Thank you to Prospero Colonna, who told me of the existence of the trunk containing the correspondence of Vittoria Colonna Caetani and who read (and corrected!) the first version of the text, sharing some aspects of the story of the house of Colonna; to him and to his sister Laurentia and brothers Marcantonio and Stefano, my gratitude for having allowed us to publish letters concerning their family.

Thank you to the heirs of Vittoria Colonna (Vittoria Bonelli Zondadari, Selina Bonelli Zondadari, Maria Aurora Misciattelli and Pietro Misciatelli) and the heirs of Umberto Boccioni (the Dal Pian-Boccionis).

Thank you to the lawyer Giovanna Cau who dealt with the question of rights; to Carlo Borromeo, who allowed me to visit his Isolino at my leisure; to Lauro Marchetti, director of the Oasi di Ninfa, who opened the way for me to the Caetani archives in the Pontine Plain; and also to Esme Howard.

Heartfelt thanks to Ester Coen for her suggestions and for having allowed me to draw on her archive; to Giovanni Aldobrandini, who, without batting an eyelid, allowed me to 'lay waste' to his library on the history of Rome; to Donata Origo, who opened the doors to what had been Vittoria Colonna's house in Rome. I thank the Museum of Vernon, Canada, which possesses many of Leone Caetani's papers; and the Library of the Accademia dei Lincei e Corsiniana which houses the papers of the Fondazione Leone Caetani di Sermoneta.

Many people have contributed—with memories, books, etc— to the writing of this book. Among them I would at least like to thank Gino Agnese, Margherita Anselmi Zondadari Scarampi di Pruney, Maura Antonelli, Carlo Barabino, Virginia Baradel, Giorgio Barba Navaretti, Cynthia Beck, Luciana Boccioni, Silvia Bonacossa Sella, Ana Luz Bravo, Domitilla Calamai, Vanna Calasso, Patrizia Cavalli, Oliva di Collobiano, Ida Corti, Grace Funk, Gelasio Gaetani Lovatelli, Milton Gendel, Raniero Gnoli, Sofia Gnoli, Alvar González-Palacios, Monica Incisa della Rocchetta, Fabio Lensini, Rosetta Loy, Carla Mattei, Barbara Melega, Benedetta Origo, Desideria Pasolini, Letizia Pasolini, Carmen Pedretti and the Office of Tourism of Verbania, Pia Pera, Gianni Pizzigoni and the Museum of Landscape in Verbania, Silvia Ronchey, Valentina Sagaria Rossi, Francesca Sanfelice, Giuseppe Scaraffia, Charles Quest-Ritson, Marco Vigevani, Linda Wills, and Luigi Zanda.

I am grateful to Fleur Jaeggy, who sought me out when she heard about this project. Thank you to Roberto Calasso and the whole of the Adelphi editorial team, as well as to Benedetta Craveri for so much generous advice. A particularly heartfelt thank you goes to Ena Marchi, the editor of this book.

Finally, I should like thank my father, Nicola Caracciolo, for his basic advice as a historian and reader, and my mother Judy, for so many things which are impossible to list. An affectionate thank you to Rossella. Thank you to my uncle Carlo and Aunt Marella, who handed on to me their fascination with gardens. Last but not least, thank you to Sandro Chia for his countless discussions of art and for his many books on Futurism. This book is dedicated to him.

Bibliography

About, Edmond, *Rome of Today*, James O Noyes, New York, 1861

Agnese, Gino, *Vita di Boccioni*, Camunia, Florence, 1996

Antonucci, Giovanni et al, *Il futurismo a Roma*, Istituto di Studi Romani, Rome, 1978

Apollinaire, Guillaume, *Apollinaire*, ed and tr Robert Chandler, Everyman, London, 2000

Ballo, Guido (ed.), *Boccioni e il suo tempo*, Arti Graphiche Fiorin, Milan, 1973

Boccioni, Umberto, *Altri inediti e apparati critici*, ed Zeno Birolli, Feltrinelli, Milan, 1972

Boccioni, Umberto, *Diari*, ed Gabriella di Milia, Abscondita, Milan, 2003

Boccioni, Umberto, *Gli scritti editi e inediti*, ed Zeno Birolli, Feltrinelli, Milan, 1971

Boccioni, Umberto, *Pittura e scultura futurista*, ed Zeno Birolli, Abscondita, Milan, 2006

Caetani, Leone, *Altri studi di storia orientale*, ed Fulvio Tessitore, L'Erma di Bretschneider, Rome, 1997

Caetani, Michelangelo, *Lettere di Michelangelo Caetani duca di Sermoneta: cultura e politica nella Roma di Pio IX*, ed Fiorella Bartoccini, Istituto di Studi Romani, Rome, 1974

Caetani, Sveva, *Recapitulation, A Journey*, ed Dennis Butler, Angela Gibbs Peart and Heidi Thompson, Coldstream Books, Vernon, 1995

Caetani, Vittoria, *Sparkle Distant Worlds*, Hutchinson & Co, London, 1947

Calvesi, Maurizio and Coen, Ester, *Boccioni. L'opera completa*, Electa, Milan, 1983

Calvesi, Maurizio, Coen, Ester and Greco, Antonella, *Boccioni prefuturista*, Electa, Milan, 1983

Caracciolo, Maria Teresa Carolina, *Memoirs by the Duchessa di San Teodoro*, Mathews & Marrot, London, 1929

Carrà, Carlo, *La mia vita*, Feltrinelli, Milan, 1981

Coen, Ester, *Umberto Boccioni*, Metropolitan Museum of Art, New York, 1988

Colonna di Sermoneta, Vittoria, *Memorie*, Fratelli Treves Editori, Milan, 1937

Futurismo e futurismi, ed Pontus Hulten, Bompiani, Milan, 1986

Gregorovius, Ferdinand, *Diari romani: 1852–1874*, Franco Spinosi Editore, Rome, 1969

Jannattoni, Livio, *Roma belle époque*, Multigrafica, Rome, 1986

L'archivio Leone Caetani all'Accademia nazionale dei Lincei, ed Paola Ghione and Valentina Sagaria Rossi, L'Erma di Bretschneider, Rome, 2004

Levi Della Vida, Giorgio, *Fantasmi ritrovati*, Neri Pozza, Venice, 1966

Marinetti, Filippo Tommaso, *Marinetti: Selected Writings*, ed R W Flint, Farrar, Straus and Giroux, New York, 1972

Mattioli Rossi, Laura (ed), *Boccioni: pittore, scultore, futurista*, Skira, Milan, 2006

Muñoz, Antonio, *Figure romane*, Staderini, Rome, 1944

Negri, Silvio, *Seconda Roma: 1850–1870*, Hoepli, Milan, 1943

Pesci, Ugo, *I primi anni di Roma capitale: 1870–1878*, Officina, Rome, 1971

Porena, Manfredi, *Roma capitale nel decennio della sua adolescenza, 1880–1890*, Edizioni di Storia e Letteratura, Rome, 1957

Rodoni, Laureto, *Tra futurismo e cultura mitteleuropea: l'incontro di Boccioni e Busoni a Pallanza*, Alberti Editore per la Società dei Verbanisti, Milan, 1998

Vasili, Paul, *Roma umbertina*, Edizioni del Borghese, Milan, 1968

Zola, Émile, *Diario romano*, Sugarco, Milan, 1989

Photographic Credits

The frontispiece and the images on pages 13, 35, 43, 53, 65, 99, 121, 145 and 185 are reproduced by kind permission of Vittoria Colonnna's great-nieces Vittoria and Selina Bonelli Zondadari.

The images on pages 75, 87, 133, 157 and 169 were found with the Boccioni-Colonna correspondence and are reproduced by kind permission of the Fondazione Camillo Caetani.

The photograph on page 27, from the collection of the Museo del Paesaggio at Verbania Pallanza, is reproduced by kind permission of Contessa Silvia Bonacossa.

The photograph on page 113, *Portrait of Ferruccio Busoni* by Umberto Boccioni, is from the Alinari Archives and is reproduced by kind permission of the Ministero per i Beni e le Attività Culturali.

The photograph on page 179 is from the Greater Vernon Museum and Archives.